The Legacy of Exile

THE NEW IMMIGRANTS SERIES

Allyn and Bacon

Series Editor, Nancy Foner, State University of New York at Purchase

Changing Identities: Vietnamese Americans, 1975–1995,
by James Freeman

*From the Workers' State to the Golden State: Jews from the
Former Soviet Union in California,* by Steven J. Gold

The Legacy of Exile: Cubans in the United States,
by Guillermo J. Grenier and Lisandro Pérez

Nuer Journeys, Nuer Lives: Sudanese Refugees in Minnesota,
by Jon Holtzman

New Pioneers in the Heartland: Hmong Life in Wisconsin,
by Jo Ann Koltyk

*From the Ganges to the Hudson: Indian Immigrants
in New York City,* by Johanna Lessinger

Salvadorans in Suburbia: Symbiosis and Conflict,
by Sarah J. Mahler

Changes and Conflicts: Korean Immigrant Families in New York,
by Pyong Gap Min

A Visa for a Dream: Dominicans in the United States,
by Patricia R. Pessar

Pride against Prejudice: Haitians in the United States,
by Alex Stepick

*Ethnicity and Entrepreneurship: The New Chinese Immigrants
in the San Francisco Bay Area,* by Bernard Wong

The Legacy of Exile: Cubans in the United States

Guillermo J. Grenier
Lisandro Pérez
Florida International University

Boston   New York   San Francisco
Mexico City   Montreal   Toronto   London   Madrid   Munich   Paris
Hong Kong   Singapore   Tokyo   Cape Town   Sydney

To our spouses
To our children
In many ways they have shared with us the legacy of exile

Series Editor: Jennifer Jacobson
Editorial Assistant: Elizabeth Lee
Marketing Manager: Taryn Wahlquist
Composition and Prepress Buyer: Linda Cox
Manufacturing Manager: Andrew Turso
Editorial-Production Coordinator: Mary Beth Finch
Editorial-Production Service: Omegatype Typography, Inc.
Electronic Composition: Omegatype Typography, Inc.

For related titles and support materials, visit our online catalog at
www.ablongman.com

Between the time Website information is gathered and then published,
it is not unusual for some sites to have closed. Also, the transcription
of URLs can result in unintended typographical errors. The publisher
would appreciate notification where these errors occur so that they
may be corrected in subsequent editions.

ISBN: 0-205-34090-3

Printed in the United States of America
10 9 8 7 6 5 4 3 2 1   07   06   05   04   03   02

Contents

Foreword to the Series...vii

Acknowledgments...ix

Two Roads to Miami: Personal Introductions.............1
   STUDYING CUBANS...2
   GRENIER'S STORY: A MINORITY OF ONE 5
   PÉREZ'S STORY: THROUGH THE
     CLASSROOM WINDOW 8
   ORGANIZATION OF THE BOOK...............................11

From Varela and Martí to Desi and Elián:
  Cuban Migration to the United States 15
   CUBAN MIGRATION TO THE UNITED STATES
     BEFORE 1959...16
   THE COLD WAR FAUCET: 1959–2000 20
   CONCLUSION: CUBAN MIGRATION AT THE
     TURN OF THE CENTURY 26

Culture: Exceptionalism, Diversity,
  and Secularism..29
   EXCEPTIONALISM..30
   DIVERSITY...35
   SECULARISM..40
   CONCLUSION 43

Miami: This Land Is Our Land 45
   "WE MADE MIAMI"..46
   "MIAMI MADE US:" CUBAN ECONOMIC SUCCESS.........48
   TYPES OF CAPITAL...51
   CONCLUSION 55

Family Business: Kinship
and Economic Adjustment 57
  MIGRATION AND FAMILY STRUCTURE 58
  "QUE PASA USA?" 60
  THE FAMILY AND ECONOMIC ADJUSTMENT 67
  CONCLUSION 68

Hanging Together, Hanging Alone: Relations
between Cubans and Others in Miami 71
  CUBANS AND THE WHITE BUSINESS ELITE:
  IT'S NOT YOUR FATHER'S CHAMBER
  OF COMMERCE 72
  AFRICAN AMERICANS AND CUBANS:
  DIVERGENT FATES 74
  CONCLUSION 81

Political Culture: The Exile Ideology
and Electoral Politics 85
  THE PERSISTENCE OF THE EXILE IDEOLOGY 86
  CURRENTS OF CHANGE 93
  PARTICIPATION IN THE U.S. POLITICAL SYSTEM 95
  CONCLUSION 98

The Trophy: Elián González and the Cuban
American Community 101
  IDENTITY AND THE LEGACY OF EXILE 107
  A WEDGE BETWEEN COMMUNITIES 109
  CONCLUSION 114

Conclusion: Exiles Much Longer? 117

References 122

Index 130

Foreword to the Series

The United States is now experiencing the largest wave of immigration in the country's history. New immigrants from Asia, Latin America, and the Caribbean are changing the American ethnic landscape.

Until recently, immigration was associated in the minds of many Americans with the massive influx of southern and eastern Europeans at the turn of the twentieth century. Since the late 1960s, America has again become a country of large-scale immigration, this time attracting newcomers from developing societies of the world, the vast majority from Asia, Mexico, Central and South America, and the Caribbean. The number of foreign-born is at an all-time high: an estimated 28.4 million immigrants were living in the United States in 2000. Although immigrants are a smaller share of the nation's population than they were at the beginning of the twentieth century—10 percent in 2000 compared to 15 percent in 1910—recent immigrants are having an especially dramatic impact because their geographic concentration is so great. In 2000, six states—California, New York, Florida, Texas, New Jersey, and Illinois—accounted for 71 percent of the immigrant population. Los Angeles, New York, Miami, San Francisco, Chicago, Washington, D.C., and Houston are, increasingly, immigrant cities with new ethnic mixes. And it is not just America's major urban centers that are experiencing immigrant inflows. Many smaller cities and towns also have growing immigrant populations.

Who are the new immigrants? What are their lives like here? How are they redefining themselves and their cultures? And how are they contributing to a new and changing America? The *New Immigrants Series* provides a set of case studies that explores these themes among a variety of groups. The books in the series are written by recognized experts who have done extensive in-depth research on particular immigrant groups. The groups represent a broad range of today's arrivals, coming from a variety of countries and cultures. The studies, based on research done in different parts of the country, cover a wide geographical range, from New York to California.

Most of the books in the series are written by anthropologists, although several sociologists are represented as well. All draw on qualitative research that shows what it means to be an immigrant in America today. As part of each study, individual immigrants tell their stories, which will help give a sense of the experiences and problems of the newcomers. Through the case studies, a dynamic picture emerges of the way immigrants are carving out new lives for themselves at the same time as they are creating a new and more diverse America.

The ethnographic case study, long the anthropologist's trademark, provides a depth often lacking in research on immigrants in the United States. Moreover, many anthropologists, like a number of authors in the *New Immigrants Series,* have done research in the country of origin as well as in the United States. Having field experience at both ends of the migration chain makes anthropologists particularly sensitive to the role of transnational ties that link immigrants to their home societies. With first-hand experience of immigrants in their home cultures, anthropologists are also well positioned to appreciate continuities as well as changes in the immigrant setting.

As immigrants become a growing presence in American society, it becomes more important than ever to learn about the newcomers and to hear their voices. The case studies in the *New Immigrants Series* will help readers understand the cultures and lives of the newest Americans and bring out the complex ways that recent immigrants are coming to terms with and creatively adapting to life in a new land.

NANCY FONER
Series Editor

Acknowledgments

We have been observing and studying Cuban Americans during our entire academic careers. There are, therefore, many people who throughout the years have contributed to enhancing our understanding and sharpening our analyses. We owe a special debt to those with whom we have had a formal collaboration on various projects. Foremost is our colleague and friend Max Castro of the North-South Center of the University of Miami, co-investigator with Grenier on the Black–Cuban relations project that provided much of the information for Chapter 6, and with whom we have both shared throughout the years so many stimulating and engaging conversations about Cubans and Miami, usually around the theme of "Is this a great town, or what?" Alex Stepick, our colleague in Florida International University's Sociology/Anthropology Department and collaborator with Grenier in the Ford Foundation's Changing Relations Project, has helped place our analyses of Cubans within the broader context of ethnicity and immigration in Miami. Much of the material on Chapter 8 on the Elián Gonzalez affair was developed as Grenier and Stepick collaborated on a forthcoming analysis of immigrants and newcomers in Miami, which continues the work initiated during the Changing Relations Project. Alex authored a monograph on Haitians in this *New Immigrants Series* and provided the critical contact with the series editor and Allyn and Bacon. Rubén Rumbaut of Michigan State and Alejandro Portes of Princeton, co-Principal Investigators of the Children of Immigrants Longitudinal Study, for which Pérez directed the fieldwork in South Florida, have contributed so much to analyzing Cubans within the context of the U.S. immigrant experience. As Cuban-born non-Miami scholars, the insights they have shared with us have been invaluable.

We consider ourselves very fortunate to be at Florida International University, where so many talented colleagues have an interest in understanding our city. Miami is a great social science laboratory, and the FIU faculty are well aware of the many opportunities and responsibilities that are inevitably and constantly created for scholars at a public university in such a dynamic urban area. There are too many to single any of them out. They know who they are and the contributions they have made to enriching our intellectual environment.

Nancy Foner, series editor, was tireless in reading drafts of the manuscript and making so many thoughtful and useful corrections and suggestions. She kept us focused and encouraged us to do our best work. We are greatly indebted to her. The staff at Allyn and Bacon were also very encouraging and helpful in the process of taking the manuscript to print.

Two Roads to Miami

Personal Introductions

Cubans are special. Not because we, the two Cuban-born authors of this book, say so, but because members of the American public say so. Many Americans love Cuban music and the fact that Desi loves Lucy, but they also recognize that there is something different about Cubans that does not fit cleanly into the Latinos-in-the-U.S.A. guide booklet. Indeed, Americans who know anything about Cubans in the United States probably know that they are not like other Latino groups—or at least that is the "official" story. Cubans (authors included, since we're also protagonists in this story) are supposedly more conservative than other Latinos and less likely to share the Civil Rights movement's penchant and passions for minority group coalition building and traditional grass roots mobilization. Cubans are cast in the role of old time Cold War warriors, obsessed with U.S. foreign policy, particularly as it relates to the resilient and enduring government of Fidel Castro. Moreover, some Americans, who admire Cuba and "real Cubans" who live on the island, look down on Cuban Americans as cultural amphibians who have created their own world in Miami.

If many Americans see Cubans as special, the fact is that the U.S. government also considered Cubans special, at least those arriving soon after the 1959 revolution. The special status of these refugees was recognized in the form of resettlement assistance, which included unique economic and social programs designed to make the exile experience less painful.

One similarity that Cubans have with other migrants to this country is that they follow others of their kind. Because of this, Cubans have settled mostly in one region of the United States: the greater Miami area, also known as Miami-Dade county. Three of every five Cuban Americans live in greater Miami. This book is focused on this community.

Of course not all Cubans live in Miami, even though, goes the saying, all might die in Miami. There are also sizable communities of

Cuban Americans in New York City and, especially, in some of the New Jersey communities that border Manhattan (West New York, Union City, Paterson, and Jersey City). Los Angeles and Chicago also have many Cubans. Take the two authors as case studies. Both came to the United States soon after the triumph of the revolution, in 1960. Both came to Miami directly from Havana with their parents. But Pérez stayed in Miami through his undergraduate education while Grenier resettled with his family in Georgia after a brief stop in West Palm Beach, where his father waited on some tables at the Belle Glades Hotel. We took different roads to the study of the Cuban American community and bring with us different perspectives.

For all the differences in our roads to Miami, we share a strong bond and commonality of purpose that sets the tone for this volume. We are Cuban American academics, analysts looking at a community that often defies analysis. Our training in U.S. academic institutions has equipped us with certain tools that allow us to peel back the surface of social reality and peer underneath. Sometimes what we find is not pretty. We do not engage in celebratory ethnocentrism. We don't smooth the contradictory edges or remove the unsightly warts. Rather, we highlight them, sometimes sympathetically, other times critically. To do otherwise would be to misrepresent our data and insult the richness and variety of the Cuban community. In fact, our training as social scientists in American academia has frequently placed us at odds with a community that flaunts its conservatism and its intolerance. The tension created by our training as academic analysts, on the one hand, and as sympathetic participants, on the other, is apparent throughout the book. As in any brief volume, we hope that this one will give rise to as many questions as it answers and that it will serve as a catalyst for readers to become even more informed about Cubans in the United States.

STUDYING CUBANS

Studying Cubans and living in Miami is much like studying magnetism and living in the North Pole. The topic is all around so you are expected to know more about it, but you still need tools to feel the forces at work. If you use those tools every day, you will have an abundance of data to help in understanding the Cuban American community. Reading *The Miami Herald* and *El Nuevo Herald* every morning would make any social scientist with our interests exclaim for all to hear "Is this a great city, or what?" Daily we are exposed to social forces in dynamic tension.

Of course, newspapers are just one source of information, and much of the material in this volume comes from collaborative research projects conducted over the years. During the late 1980s and early 1990s, Grenier was involved with the Ford Changing Relations Project (CRP), which explored the nature and consequences of daily interactions among members of various ethnic communities in Miami-Dade County, including Cubans (see Lamphere 1992; Lamphere et. al. 1994; Stepick et. al. forthcoming). We have both continued ethnographic work throughout the 1990s, exploring ethnic relations and political dynamics in Miami. Grenier has worked closely with anthropologist Alex Stepick and sociologist Max Castro in some of the research presented in this volume, particularly in Chapters 6 and 8. Throughout the 1990s, the authors have conducted interviews and engaged in participant observation in scores of homes, workplaces, schools, and organizations as well as in dozens of private meetings with policy makers and community leaders.

Pérez has been analyzing U.S. census data on the Cuban-origin population ever since the release of the results of the 1970 decennial census. His focus has been mainly on sociodemographic characteristics and the Cuban American family, but he has also been interested in U.S. policy toward Cuba and the impact of Cuban Americans on the development of that policy. More recently, he conducted fieldwork in South Florida for the Children of Immigrants Longitudinal Study, directed by Alejandro Portes and Rubén Rumbaut. His analysis of the results of the subsample of Cuban-origin children (1,242 cases) appears in one of the project's recent publications (Pérez 2001).

We also draw on the findings of our Florida International University Cuba Poll, the only regularly conducted scientific survey of the attitudes of the Cuban American community in Miami toward the island. Conducting this poll every two years since 1991 has given us a sense of the persistence of the exile identity within the community as well as the changing nature of that identity. Unlike many other surveys, the Cuba Poll has had enviably low refusal rates. Cubans are eager to talk about Cuba, and we have been eager to listen.

Ultimately, we have learned a great deal about the Cuban American experience by simply listening and observing everyday life in a dynamic community. We listen and observe shopping at "El Publix" as the elderly bag "boy" tells a customer a story about fishing off Havana's Malecón for real fresh fish, "not this frozen trash that nobody knows where it came from." We listen and watch as the two attendants behind the counter at a clothing store see a blonde customer entering and remark, "here comes una Americana," and are surprised when the Americana answers, "Yes. You have a problem with that?" in near perfect Spanish. We hear the responses to our knocks when we arrive exactly on time at a Cuban party: "Hurry up. Someone is here already. Must be one of the Americans you invited." We observe the tension created when only one office worker does not understand

Spanish and is excluded from most conversations. Teaching at a university with more undergraduate students of Cuban origin than the University of Havana, we never tire of the enthusiasm with which our Cuban American students approach the subject of Cuba—although we also cringe at the many myths they have inherited from their parents about the island and its people. As consultants and advisors we have had the opportunity to work with community leaders at all levels and to observe the tensions between the old guard cold warriors and the moderate *dialogueros* in community meetings, board rooms, union halls, and workplaces, as well as in political arenas.

The great sociologist C. Wright Mills introduced the concept of the *sociological imagination* into our analytical toolbox.

> Neither the life of an individual nor the history of a society can be understood without understanding both. Yet men do not usually define the troubles they endure in terms of historical change and institutional contradiction.... The sociological imagination enables its possessor to understand the larger historical scene in terms of its meaning for the inner life and the external career of a variety of individuals.... The first fruit of this imagination—and the first lesson of the social science that embodies it—is the idea that the individual can understand his own experience and gauge his own fate only by locating himself within this period, that he can know his own chances in life only by becoming aware of those of all individuals in his circumstances.... We have come to know that every individual lives, from one generation to the next, in some society; that he lives out a biography, and that he lives it out within some historical sequence (Mills 1959, pp. 3–6).

These ideas are tailor-made for the Cuban American analyst of the Cuban American experience in the United States. Like other Cubans, we are all protagonists with biographies that intersect with the history of the community. Yet, as academics, we are also analysts who have tried to step back and go beyond our individual lives to provide a broader understanding of the Cuban migration and the creation of a Cuban community in Miami.

Because this book is so deeply rooted in our role as participant analysts, we think it is important to include some background on the different roads that led us to Miami and to this book. Telling our stories is not an exercise in narcissism, but an appropriate introduction to the rest of the book. These are the biographies that sparked our sociological imaginations and led us to analyze the larger social landscape. Since the Cuban migrant community has such a tumultuous and polemic history, it is important to know not just what is being said but who is saying it, and where they are coming from. These are our personal narratives of the roads we traveled to reach this book.

GRENIER'S STORY: A MINORITY OF ONE

The last memories that I have of Cuba are too corny to relate but I will anyway. They're of me riding in a car, on my knees looking out the back seat at the waving figures of my aunts and uncles, the ones who got to stay. I wished that I was staying. I waved back. The image that I've always had of the moment is one of stick figures stiffly waving and disappearing in the distance. I was vaguely aware of my sister next to me on the seat but not much else. I don't remember the airports or the tearful farewells that my parents say occurred. I'll take their word for it. I also don't remember my mother, the night before departure, stuffing hundred dollar bills down the handle of our umbrellas or inside the buttons of the winter coats that we would use in Miami. I'll take their word for that too.

That was on November 6, 1960, almost two years after the triumph of the revolution. As a nine-year-old kid whose biggest worry was not to get a sea anemone stuck in his foot as he waded into the rocky shores of Cojímar, outside of Havana, the Revolution was a distant event brought home by the discussions at the dinner table and rumors in the streets. At the dinner table I understood that the revolution was a good thing for some and not for others. Both of my parents, particularly my father, supported the *guerrilleros*. My mother was always more suspicious, perhaps influenced by her mother, a Gallega who had immigrated to Cuba at the turn of the century with a Gallego husband from the rural northwest region of Spain. Cuba was the land of opportunity for them and they made the most of it by establishing one of the first automotive repair shops in Havana. My grandmother always suspected that the revolution was *comunista*.

One of those alleged *comunistas* walked down the streets of Cojímar one day handing out bullets as souvenirs to the kids. I also remember taking one that dropped to the ground rather than going up to him as the others were doing. He was an imposing figure in his fatigues and long black beard. I heard later that his name was Camilo Cienfuegos.

My father's family had deep roots in the island. He could count at least one Mambí (a member of the Cuban independence army) in the known family tree, and my father himself was active as a student in political affairs. All this made him a bit more hopeful about the revolution and its consequences.

So I was surprised when I found out that we were leaving, even though my parents tried to hide the significance of the move. It will just be for a little while, they said, a vacation like others we had taken in Miami. That rang true enough. Miami was the preferred vacation spot for many middle class Cubans, I found out later. I also found out later that in Cuba, I was middle class.

Class standing didn't transfer well to our new home in the United States. My father was unable to find a permanent job in Miami, so we moved to West Palm Beach, where he worked for few months for a Cuban airline agency until it closed in early 1961. Eventually, he settled in as a waiter at the Sea Breeze Hotel. This was not an easy transition for a person who had hopes of retiring with a decent pension while still young enough to enjoy it.

My parents tried to shelter me as much as they could from the difficulties of exile. Christmas in West Palm was a particularly difficult time. My mother found a nativity scene at a local Woolworth's for ninety-seven cents and has put it up every Christmas since. My sister and I saw few gifts, and those that we did see were from acquaintances who felt sorry for us.

I attended Saint Michael's Catholic School while in West Palm. One of my classmates was a Cuban whose family owned the largest sugar mills in Florida. I spoke little English so he was entrusted with the task of translating to the teacher my answers and comments. Language learning being what it is, I could understand much earlier than I could speak. I remember the frustration of understanding him as he knowingly gave erroneous information to the teacher. He carried his teasing and intimidation to the playground, where I found myself isolated from him and other students. So much for ethnic solidarity.

During this time my parents burnt the midnight oil writing letters to colleges asking for positions as language instructors. They didn't know anything about searching for academic positions in the United States. They used the public library and identified two hundred colleges, mostly in the South, because of the warm weather and proximity to Cuba. Over two hundred letters went out and fewer than five responses came back. In July 1961 we packed our Chevrolet 1955 station wagon and headed for Gainesville, Georgia, where my father would begin his career as a faculty member at Brenau College, a private girls' school and I would begin my career as a minority of one in the Gainesville Public School System.

The years passed. I remember what I was doing when Kennedy was assassinated and I remember seeing the cover of the first Beatles album before seeing them on Ed Sullivan. I played football and ran track. I tried to date girls who intimidated me. I drank beer on weekends and hung out at the Dairy Queen. I was for all intents and purposes as American as any other teenage boy growing up in the semi-rural south.

I also remember the Vietnam War and the Civil Rights movement. The culture of the period was thick with issues of social justice and injustice. During high school I managed to ignore the rumblings until I turned 18 and the draft lottery was introduced. As the possibility loomed that my birth date might be drawn early from the hat and that I would have to enlist, my parents panicked. "One of the reasons we left Cuba was because Fidel wanted to send our kids to Russia and into the army," said my mother, "No way that we're going to let the United States take you and send you to Vietnam." The possibility of moving to Canada was explored but, thankfully, my number came up in the lottery only after 300 had been drawn before me.

The Civil Rights movement became more obvious to me when I attended college in Atlanta. It never occurred to me that others might prejudge me because of my background. I always thought that dislike was based on personal attributes. Watching the African American struggle in Atlanta made me aware of the injustices inherent in the "land of the free and the home of the brave." It made me painfully aware of the tainted history of the southern culture that I had been so eager to call my own in high school.

All this while, Cuba receded in the rearview mirror. It was my parents' land but I had my hands full with this one. I listened to Jimi Hendrix way before I listened to Beni Moré.

It was only after college graduation, when I enrolled in Latin American Studies program at the University of New Mexico, that I began to really learn about Cuba. I learned about the revolution, its goals and aspirations. I learned about its defiance of the U.S. government and its alliance with progressive forces throughout the world. It seemed to me that my parents had fled the wrong oppressor. This sense that I had been raised in the *entrañas del monstro* ("the entrails of the monster") to quote José Martí, and that all things Cuban, from the island, were superior to the arrogance of power practiced by the U.S. government drove an ambiguous wedge between me and my family. They did not love the U.S. government but appreciated its welcome. They loved Cuba but hated its government and the exile it had imposed on them. The fact that I wanted to get closer to the culture of the island pleased them, but they strongly objected to the idea of my traveling there.

But travel I did, and I began to study Cuba and class struggles throughout Latin America. A twist of fate redirected my attention to class struggles in the United States and how labor organizations attempt to represent the interests of the working class. This led to a dissertation that was published as a book and in 1985 a position as Director of the Center for Labor Research and Studies at Florida International University in Miami.

I thought that I knew about Miami and its Cubans. I had read the literature and envisioned a monolithic enclave of right-wing zealots. How wrong I was became evident the first day in my new position when I was treated to lunch by two Cuban American leaders of American labor unions. There was more class and ideological diversity within the Cuban community than I had ever imagined. Before I knew it, I was immersed in an incredibly rich and militant community whose ideals of social justice ran deep. While I still usually find myself in the minority in gatherings of Cubans when discussing the U.S. embargo and other political issues relating to Cuba, I am no longer a minority of one.

PÉREZ'S STORY: THROUGH THE CLASSROOM WINDOW

I woke up early on New Year's Day 1959 to hear my father say: "The man left." What strikes me now as remarkable is that although I was only ten years old, I knew exactly what my father meant. I knew the man was Fulgencio Batista. I knew why he left and I had some notion—as much as anyone in Cuba—of what was supposed to happen next. I felt—as did most of the island—that this was good news.

I can pinpoint precisely the place and time when I started developing my acute awareness of the historic conflict unfolding around me. The place was Lafayette School, a private bilingual American school on Fifth Avenue in the Havana suburb of Miramar, on the second floor, the classroom with the big windows. The time was the afternoon of October 29, 1956, during English reading class, third grade. I was seven years old.

Lafayette was the only school I would ever attend in Cuba. I was there, and not in a Catholic school like most of my contemporaries, because my father wanted me to learn English. He became fluent in the language after spending five years in (and graduating from) a private prep school in New York. His father never learned English, but appreciated its importance in a Cuba in which the investments, the business, the tourists, the cars, and the refrigerators, in short, everything, or so it seemed, came from *El Norte*. So my father and three of his brothers were sent to Woodmere Academy in Long Island. My grandfather wanted his children to do what he could never do during his long and successful career as a tobacco exporter: speak directly to the people in New York who each year bought from him large quantities of quality tobacco leaves grown in central Cuba.

That October afternoon in 1956 my classmates and I were taking turns reading aloud in class about how maple syrup is produced in Vermont. I was engrossed in this exotic story, glancing at the pictures of the maple forest blanketed with snow, when I heard loud popping noises. They were coming from very near the school.

The reader stopped in midsentence and we all looked at the teacher, a middle-aged American woman with dark red hair. Her face did not give me any reassurance. I felt a prickling sensation run up my spine. She asked me and two others sitting by the window to move our desks toward the center of the classroom. After a few seconds of uncertainty, she started reading aloud about maple syrup and ordered the class to follow along in the book. The shots multiplied, cars were speeding and screeching along Fifth Avenue, and police sirens could be heard everywhere. We were having a hard time keeping our minds in Vermont.

After what seemed an eternity, everything stopped. I made it my business to find out what happened and why. The Haitian embassy, a stone's throw from my school, had been attacked by the police. Armed men had taken refuge in the embassy, and the police suspected that one of them had been responsible for the assassination of a government official two days earlier. The police chief and many others were killed in the attack.

As it turned out, that event signaled the beginning of the intensification of the violent conflict that would eventually overthrow the Batista government. During the months and years to follow, the violence, the explosions, the gunshots, the victims, would multiply. I was not yet ten, but I became accustomed to carefully reading every newspaper and magazine that entered my house. Something was going on out there that affected me, and I wanted to know what it was. Eventually Batista left, only to give way to a new cycle of unrest and uncertainty. My parents had sympathized with the revolution at the beginning. But by the middle of 1960 they felt certain that their world was changing in a way they found threatening, that their lives were on the verge of being profoundly transformed.

On October 29, 1960, four years to the day after my reading on maple syrup was interrupted, I clutched my little brother's hand and boarded an airplane for Miami. I did not know when I would return to Cuba again. The news my father had given me on that New Year's Day had turned out to be not so good after all.

My parents decided to settle in Miami, where I would live for the next ten years. In Cuba, my father had always either worked for his father or had his own business, so when he arrived in Miami he could not envision any other option but self-employment. He had no capital, but he did have one great asset. His father, by this time deceased, could not have known in 1933, when he packed him off to New York, just how critical it would be for his son to learn English well. My father went into direct sales, and during the next fifteen years he walked the sidewalks of Hialeah, a working class suburb of

Miami, as a Fuller Brush salesman, strictly on commission. At the time, Hialeah was a predominantly white English-speaking community, but with a growing Cuban presence. He could sell in two languages, and he sold enough to support his family.

In Miami I was in a community obsessed with Cuba, but more importantly for me, a community that shared my sense that I was not supposed to be there. I was suddenly no longer in Lafayette School, but in an unfamiliar school, with classmates I did not know, in a strange city. It was as if someone had made a big mistake.

I never stopped reading the newspaper. I had already learned that political events could have an impact on one's life. My passions were current events and history, but those were not professions. I was going to be a lawyer. During my undergraduate years at the University of Miami, I realized, however, that my professors made a living from studying things like history, politics, society, and culture. That's what I wanted to do. My life had been determined by those larger forces. I had developed what Mills referred to as part of the sociological imagination: the ability to see the intersection of history and biography.

At the University of Miami I also had the opportunity to be active in Cuban student politics. I was editor of the occasional newspaper of the Cuban student organization, a strongly anti-Castro publication. I participated in demonstrations and rallies against the Cuban government. But by the time I graduated, it was clear that my relationship with Cuba would not be political, but rather one in which I would pursue the road of analysis and understanding. I would be a sociologist and try to understand how and why history had so clearly intersected my biography.

I left Miami for graduate school in Gainesville, Florida, and then to my first academic job at Louisiana State University. I was away from the political world of Cuban Miami for fifteen years, which helped me to develop the analytical and critical eye of an outsider. I learned that there are many realities to the world of Cuba and Cuban Americans. In 1979 the possibility of returning to Cuba for a visit first came up, and I seized on the opportunity and have been visiting ever since.

When in 1985 Florida International University offered me a position as Chair of its Sociology and Anthropology Department, and with it the opportunity to return to Miami, I jumped at the chance. I was ready to return to a place where my work on Cuba and Cuban Americans would have more resonance, if not always a welcome. Most of my Cuban colleagues around the country thought it was a mistake. It would not be possible, they told me, to do serious academic work on Cuba in the land of exiles.

To be sure, it has not been easy. A passionate and political community of exiles does not expect analysis from one of its own. It expects loyalty to its cause. I have been roundly and routinely criticized in the vitriolic press of Cuban Miami for my writings and for my commitment to contact and openness with Cuba. The FBI once had reason to place surveillance on my house for my protection.

But it has been worthwhile. Cuban Miami has changed in a way that is more hospitable to pluralism. It is rare that an academic gets to do work that is so clearly relevant to the surrounding social milieu. I am teaching students to understand and interpret what is happening right outside our classroom. In that sense, my world as a professor in Miami at the beginning of the twenty-first century shares at least one characteristic with the world of my childhood in Havana midway through the previous century: the doings of my people continue to drift in through the classroom window.

ORGANIZATION OF THE BOOK

In this volume, we attempt to give a broad vision of the Cuban community in the United States. We present multiple voices and a variety of points of view. Cubans are not a monolithic entity. All are not conservative; all are not obsessed with Cuba. In fact, all are not anything, except Cuban or Cuban American. That is the only descriptor that is completely accurate. Using that as the highest common denominator, we cover the major themes in the Cuban American story.

In Chapter 2 we present an overview of the various waves of migration from Cuba to the United States from the mid-nineteenth century to the close of the twentieth century. We emphasize the long tradition of emigration in response to political events in the island as well as the establishment of communities that have focused extensively on the homeland. The tradition of nineteenth-century expatriates, such as Felix Varela and Jose Martí, as well as the creation and development of the Florida cigar-making communities, are explored, as well as the characteristics, settlement patterns, and integration of those earlier waves. We highlight, of course, the post-1959 waves and the role of political events and decisions in regulating the flow and characteristics of the migrants during the past forty years.

Chapter 3, on cultural contributions, starts with the distinctive nature of Cuban culture itself, described more than sixty years ago by the ethnographer Fernando Ortiz as the result of intricate and countless "transculturations." Miami reflects that very vibrant culture of the island in its music and religious traditions, clearly African and Spanish in origins, but distinctly Cuban in their juxtaposition. The chapter also deals with the sense of exceptionalism that these cultural roots imbue in the average Cuban and how this uniqueness shapes Cuban identity.

Chapter 4 presents one of the most salient characteristics of the Cuban American community in Miami: its economic adjustment. The chapter traces how the socioeconomic selectivity of the 1960s' migration translated into the creation of a true ethnic enclave in Miami, thereby shaping the social, political, cultural, and economic institutions of this "frontier" city and paving the way for the integration of more recent arrivals. We focus on the dynamics and consequences of the enclave. The chapter establishes the basis for the next three chapters, which explore some of the positive and negative consequences of the enclave.

Chapter 5 analyzes how the high incidence of family-based entrepreneurship has contributed to the rise of the enclave. The Cuban family in Miami is organized in a manner that supports upward social mobility: high rates of female labor force participation, a relatively large number of workers per family, low fertility, and more than two generations in the household. Kin-based networks represent a major factor in the spread of entrepreneurship and the accumulation of capital that have characterized the enclave and the Cuban "success story."

The enclave has had a major impact on interethnic relations in the Miami area. Immigrants' insulation within the enclave may have positive implications for economic adjustment, but poorly serves interethnic communications and understanding. Chapter 6 deals with the issues confronting the Cuban American community in relationships with other groups in Miami, especially African Americans and Caribbean Blacks.

Chapter 7 focuses on the pervasiveness and persistence of an exile ethos within the Cuban community. The insularity of the enclave, and its media and leadership, have combined to keep the anti-Castro struggle not only alive but also an overriding consideration within Cuban Miami, affecting even the conduct of local matters. The recovery of the homeland remains an emotional issue and one that is largely unquestioned. Nevertheless, the Cuban community's political culture is not totally monolithic, as many Cuban Americans have recently voiced other perspectives on the relationship with the homeland and some travel frequently to the island to visit family.

Treating the saga of Elián González as a case study, Chapter 8 demonstrates how the story of the little boy summarizes and illustrates much of what has been said previously in the book, especially in terms of the enclave and political culture. The remaining standard bearers of the "exile ideology" were able to define the destiny of Elián as a political battle to be waged against Fidel Castro, placing them at odds with most of the United States, which saw the saga as a family reunification issue. The Elián case served to reaffirm a Cuban identity among younger Cuban Americans; it also affected the image of Cubans held by non-Cubans in the United States. It tells us a great deal about the present and future development of Cuban Miami.

In the concluding Chapter 9 we venture some thoughts on the future of the Cuban American community in the United States. Will Cuban Americans continue to consider themselves exiles even as the generation of the revolution (here and in Cuba) dies off, or will they become another ethnic group contributing to the "Hispanization" of the United States?

2

From Varela and Martí to Desi and Elián

Cuban Migration to the United States

On December 15, 1823, during a heavy blizzard, the ship *Draper C. Thorndike* sailed into New York's harbor from Gibraltar. It carried salt, almonds, and a handful of passengers. Among them was a Cuban priest named Félix Varela, a prominent figure in the nascent movement to free Cuba from Spanish control. The story goes that shortly after disembarking, Varela slipped and fell on an icy Manhattan street. As he was being helped up by friends and former students who greeted him at the dock, one of them jokingly told the priest that there was a legend in New York that predicted that all foreigners who fell on the snow when they arrived were destined to spend the rest of their lives in the city (Hernández Travieso 1984, 292). The priest must have thought the prediction amusing and very far-fetched. After all, he was only thirty-five years old and found himself in New York almost by accident. The *Thorndike* happened to be the first ship out of Gibraltar after Varela had to literally flee Spain when his pleas for greater Cuban autonomy were violently rejected by the Spanish monarch, Ferdinand VII, who proceeded to imprison and execute those who sought liberal reforms (McCadden and McCadden 1984, 49). Varela probably regarded New York only as a way station until he could return to his native island.

But the legend became reality, as Varela would spend the next thirty years of his life in lower Manhattan, establishing parishes and ministering to his flock of poor immigrants, most of them Irish. He never returned to Cuba.

Félix Varela, as a prominent Cuban separatist, could be regarded as the first person with a Cuban (not Spanish) identity who lived in the United States. As such, the arrival of the *Thorndike* on that day in 1823 represents the beginning of the story of Cubans in the United

States. It is fitting that the story start with Varela, for his experience established the theme of the Cuban presence in this country, a theme that would be echoed by virtually every wave of Cubans that has come to the United States since that winter day in 1823.

As with Varela's arrival, all major waves of Cuban immigrants throughout the nineteenth and twentieth centuries have been triggered by political conditions in the island. It is an immigration that cannot be understood without reference to its political and policy contexts. Like Varela, Cubans have arrived in the United States as "reluctant migrants," defining themselves as exiles who await the opportunity to return and recover the island from the political order that compelled them to leave. Many did return, but most shared Varela's fate, spending the rest of their days without ever seeing their island again. The legacy of exile has punctuated the Cuban presence in the United States.

CUBAN MIGRATION TO THE UNITED STATES BEFORE 1959

It is widely recognized that the contemporary Cuban presence in the United States is linked to the conditions created by the revolution of 1959. The flow of Cubans to the United States, however, dates back to Varela, and although that earlier immigration never reached the levels of the post-1959 exodus, it should not be overlooked. Varela and the other early immigrants established the tradition of Cuban political exile in the United States, creating a well-worn path that would be heavily used by those leaving a socialist Cuba.

New York's Nineteenth-Century Exiles

Francisco Vicente Aguilera, scion of a wealthy and aristocratic family from eastern Cuba, must have been quite a sight on the streets of Manhattan in the 1870s. Sporting a long gray beard and trudging in the snow with worn boots and frayed clothes, he was constantly making the rounds of those New Yorkers who might contribute to Cuba's independence from Spain (Portuondo 1975, 395). A war for that independence had broken out in 1868 and Aguilera agreed to represent the Cuban insurrectionists in New York, organizing the exiles and raising money. He had given up his patrician life and made every sacrifice so that he could return to a Cuba free from Spanish control, but he never returned. Aguilera died in New York in 1877. One year later, the war for the independence of Cuba ended without accomplishing its purpose.

Aguilera and Varela were not the only Cubans who walked New York's cold streets during the nineteenth century, vainly expecting a return to an independent Cuba. The struggle to oust Spain was an arduous and protracted one, lasting from the early stirrings of separatism of Varela's time to the armed conflicts that started in 1868 and 1895 and culminated in the Spanish-Cuban-American War of 1898 and the subsequent U.S. occupation of the island. The Cubans would have to wait until the twentieth century, 1902, before they could finally have their own government.

The severely autocratic nature of Spanish rule created an important presence of exiles in the United States, and it was in this country, especially in New York, that many important chapters of Cuban history were written (Poyo 1989). In the decades after Varela arrived in 1823, almost every prominent Cuban separatist found himself at one time or another in New York in response to the political situation in Cuba (Pérez 1994a, 160–161). In 1870, the year of the first decennial U.S. census that tabulated the Cuban-born separately, New York City (including Brooklyn) had 1,565 Cubans, by far the largest of all concentrations of Cubans in the United States. In 1880, the census counted more than 2,000 Cubans in that city (Pérez 2000, 17).

That year opened with an event that would in time prove pivotal to New York's Cuban community. On January 3, 1880, a day not much warmer than the one that greeted Father Varela fifty-seven years before, the most important figure in Cuban history arrived in New York harbor. The *France*'s manifest shows that "Mr. Martí" boarded at Le Havre, that he traveled in second class, and that he was twenty-six years of age, an "advocate" by occupation, and a citizen of Spain (U.S. National Archives and Records Service 1958). The young lawyer must have slipped on an icy Manhattan street upon arrival, for the legend that haunted Varela also plagued him: he would spend the next fifteen years living in New York, returning to his native Cuba only five weeks before his violent death on a battlefield.

José Martí is regarded as the intellectual architect of the modern Cuban nation. Through his essays, letters, and speeches he crafted the ideals upon which Cubans should construct a sovereign country. More importantly, he forged the political movement that in 1895 launched the final and definitive armed struggle for the independence of Cuba. All of this he accomplished almost entirely during those fifteen years he was an exile in New York City. That he was able to achieve so much in those years is a testament not only to his abilities, but to the size and political activism of the Cuban community in New York and throughout the United States, which backed the efforts of the articulate young revolutionary to build a new nation.

The Florida Cigarmaking Communities

Among Martí's staunchest supporters were Cuban cigarworkers in the United States. The ten-year conflict that started in 1868 had disastrous consequences for the economy of the island. Cigar manufacturers found it increasingly difficult to maintain normal business operations, especially since the Spanish government had placed high tariffs on all exported tobacco products. Many relocated their factories to New York and Key West. Their employees followed them there and by the 1870s both communities had a sizable number of cigarworkers.

One of the cigar manufacturers who left the island was the owner of a well-known brand, *El Príncipe de Gales*, Vicente Martínez Ybor. Although Spanish-born, he had arrived as a youngster in Cuba and had pro-Cuban sentiments. Not along after the outbreak of hostilities in 1868, Martínez Ybor found himself in a precarious position, not only as a businessman in a deteriorating economic climate, but also as a persecuted conspirator against Spain. He barely escaped arrest, fleeing in a schooner to Key West, the southernmost point of the Florida Keys, just ninety miles from Cuba.

The hot and humid climate of Key West was similar to Cuba's, ideal for the manufacture of cigars. Relocation to the United States had two additional advantages: a stable political situation and low tariffs on the importation of tobacco leaves. By 1870, Key West was a boom-town and a leading center for cigar manufacturing in the United States. The census that year counted more than 1,000 persons born in Cuba (Pérez 2000, 17). Only New York had a larger Cuban community. The importance of the Cuban presence in Key West was felt immediately, as the new immigrants combined their activism for Cuban independence with participation in local politics. A Cuban was elected mayor in 1876 and eventually Cubans would occupy positions as county judges, city commissioners, and representatives to the state legislature (Castellanos 1935, 176). Martínez Ybor's cigar manufacturing business flourished in Key West, but Key West had the disadvantage of not having a direct rail connection to New York, the distribution center for his cigars. Furthermore, his workers on the small island were becoming increasingly attracted to something Martínez Ybor found intolerable: labor unions. By the 1880s he was looking to move to a location that would offer better transportation links to New York, yet be small enough so that it could be developed into a "company town," following the model used by other industries in the U.S. Midwest to keep out labor organizers. He settled on a perfect location: Tampa, a fishing village located on a harbor on Florida's Gulf coast. In 1885, with financial incentives offered by the local Board of Trade, Martínez Ybor bought forty acres northeast of

Tampa, enough land to build not only cigar factories, but an entire town (Westfall 1977, 61–63). It would be known as Ybor City and it would rapidly become the largest nineteenth-century community of Cuban Americans.

In the spring of 1886, the first two cigar factories in Ybor City were nearing completion: Martínez Ybor's own *El Príncipe de Gales* and *La Flor de Sánchez y Haya*, the factory of his partner in the Ybor City project, Ignacio Haya. The politics of the homeland, however, determined that Haya's factory would have the honor of producing Ybor city's first cigar on April 13. The workers at *El Príncipe de Gales* went on strike even before the factory opened to protest the hiring of a Spanish bookkeeper (Mormino and Pozzetta 1987, 66). The cigar-makers had come to Ybor City to work, but apparently that did not mean that they ceased to act as exiles, giving priority to Cuba's political situation.

Eventually, of course, Martínez Ybor's factory opened, and many other cigar manufacturers also established their businesses in Ybor City. Besides factories, the community included housing for workers, social clubs, restaurants, health clinics, and stores. Ybor City grew rapidly. One indication of its growing importance is that Martí, during his organizing and fundraising campaign, visited the community from New York no less than nine times between 1891 and 1894. He found tremendous support among the cigarmakers for the cause of independence. Once the armed struggle erupted in Cuba in 1895, even more cigarmakers migrated to the United States in response to the political conditions in the island and Ybor City became a hotbed of revolutionary activity (Rivero Muñiz 1958, 77–105). By the census of 1900, Ybor City had more Cuban-born residents than New York and it would continue to grow: the 1910 U.S. census counted more than 6,000 Cuban-born persons in the community (Pérez 2000, 18). By that time, however, a combination of forces were already underway that would eventually determine Ybor City's decline as a major Cuban American community.

The end of Spanish rule in Cuba, followed by a U.S. occupation and the establishment of the Cuban Republic in 1902, ushered in an era in which political stability was essentially guaranteed by the United States through the Platt Amendment, a provision of the Cuban Constitution of 1901 that, among other things, gave the United States the right to intervene to maintain a stable government that would "protect life, property, and individual liberty" (Pérez 1988, 186). The armed struggle and unfavorable business climate that compelled Martínez Ybor and many others to leave Cuba decades earlier were in the past at the start of the new century. Ybor City's cigar manufacturers were also facing a deteriorating situation as both labor conflicts and tariffs increased. The independence struggle had served to unite the manufacturers and cigarmakers in a common political cause. The end of the struggle, however, allowed long-standing labor-management grievances to surface. Strikes and lockouts started as early as 1899. The once-favorable tariff situation started changing rapidly in the early 1900s as the lobbying in Congress by the U.S. Tobacco Trust resulted in higher tariffs on the importation of tobacco leaves. The Trust, composed of U.S. cigar manufacturers that used domestic tobacco, regarded Ybor City as a great threat, for the Tampa product was made with fine imported Cuban leaves (Westfall 1977, 95–98). The new tariffs largely removed the competitive edge that Ybor City had enjoyed over the Cuban-made product, as well as over other cigars made in the United States.

In short, the factors that gave rise to the Florida cigarmaking communities were no longer present at the dawn of the twentieth century. The Depression, mechanization of cigar production, and the growing popularity of cigarettes dealt the final death blows to the manufacture in the United States of fine cigars handmade from Cuban tobacco. All of these conditions favored the return of the industry to Havana. By 1930, the Cuban-born population of Ybor City had declined to the point where New York regained its historical primacy as the most important Cuban American community.

During the Depression and World War II, Cuban immigration to the United States reached all-time lows. Nevertheless, the close economic, cultural, and political relationship between the United States and Cuba resulted in substantial travel between the two countries. Americans went to the island for business and pleasure, and Cubans came to the United States on a temporary basis seeking to develop their careers, either in U.S. schools, in music, in the entertainment industry, or in professional sports, notably baseball and boxing (Pérez 1994a, 184–8). Yet the political factor was not entirely absent even in this period. Three Cuban presidents and members of their governments felt compelled to leave Cuba for the United States after abandoning power. The first of them, Gerardo Machado, Cuba's first dictator, arrived in 1933 and spent the rest of his life in the United States. He is buried in Miami next to a friend, the mayor of Santiago de Cuba during his administration, who also left the island after Machado's ouster. The mayor was accompanied to the United States by his musically-talented teenage son, who would become a successful bandleader, a Cuban American icon, and a familiar face on American television: Desiderio (Desi) Arnaz, Jr. (Pérez Firmat 1994, 48–76).

THE COLD WAR FAUCET: 1959–2000

During the second half of the twentieth century, migration from socialist Cuba was one of the longest-running human dramas on the world stage. A seemingly interminable saga that has spanned more than forty years and continues into the twenty-first century, the exodus has provided the world with scenes of tragedy, desperation, courage, mendacity, absurdity, and even farce and comedy. It has been a surreal and incredulous drama with one major theme: the drastic and irreversible impact of political forces on individual human lives. Of the countless stories that have emerged from this protracted show, here is a sampler that illustrates the range of experiences generated since it all started in 1959:

- Nine-year old María Teresa Carrera and her brother were sent to the United States by their parents, who remained in Cuba. They were received in this country by strangers who cared for them. Their parents told the children they would be following them as soon as they could. Nearly two years would elapse before their parents could join them in the United States. The Carrera siblings were two of more than 14,000 school-aged children who migrated unaccompanied between December 1960 and October 1962. Their parents sent them ahead because they were fearful about their children's future under the new revolution. They were cared for in the United States largely by religious organizations and foster parents until their parents could leave Cuba. Many children waited much longer for their parents than did the Carreras (Triay 1998, 71–72).

- *The Miami Herald* reporter was struck by Ibis Guerrero's stoicism during the funeral in Key West. The 14-year-old was her family's sole survivor when the *Olo Yumi*, a 36-foot boat loaded with fifty-two Cubans sank in the Florida Straits on its way to the United States. Ibis was determined not to share a tear because "so many people have already died." She kept her word as she watched the burial of her entire family: mother, father, grandmother, and two sisters. Nine other people on the boat drowned. The *Olo Yumi* was one of 2,011 boats that between April 20 and September 29, 1980 took part in what became know as the Mariel boatlift, transporting 125,266 persons from the port of Mariel in Cuba to Key West. Without any relatives in the United States, it was not clear who would care for Ibis (Rivas 1980, 10).

- Eugenio Maderal Román reached Marathon Key, Florida, on February 8, 1994, after reportedly windsurfing the 110 miles from Cuba (Lisandro Pérez 1999, 201).

- On January 31, 1996, Margarita Uría Sánchez, 33, clutched a statue of the Virgin of Charity as she boarded a Boeing 727 airliner at the U.S. Naval Base in Guantánamo, Cuba, for a flight to Homestead Air Force Base in southern Florida. She was the last of the more than 31,000 Cubans who, since August 1994, had made their home in a makeshift tent camp at the Guantánamo base. Margarita was one of some 35,000 rafters who left Cuba in less than a month in 1994 and were interdicted by the Coast Guard and sent to Guantánamo. They were classified by the U.S. government as "excludables." But most of them, like Margarita, were eventually admitted into the United States (Lisandro Pérez 1999, 207).

These extraordinary stories, and countless others, have been made possible by an equally extraordinary political climate that has remained virtually unchanged over more than four decades. At the core of that political context has been Cuba's radical transformation into a country with a centrally-planned economy with virtually no private industry and a government organized along Marxist-Leninist principles, along with close ties to, and dependence upon, the former Soviet Union.

Such a transformation resulted in a conflict that was most intense in the early 1960s, but which has lasted to this day. It is a conflict that originated over competing economic, political, and ideological systems and inextricably combined an internal class struggle with an international Cold War confrontation. In that conflict, both the U.S. government and various sectors of Cuban society, especially the elites, virtually all of which went into exile, have shared a strong interest in overthrowing the Cuban government, and have cooperated in a number of ways towards that end. Internally, the situation in Cuba has been characterized by economic austerity, at times severe, and by an inflexible authoritarian political system that has refused to institute needed economic and political reforms.

The most visible and recurring manifestation of the Cuban saga over the past four decades has been emigration. The waves of migration from the island since 1960 have all taken place within that enduring climate of hostility and international confrontation. Although those waves have differed a great deal from each other in their specific conditions and characteristics, they have all been the result of an international conflict that has utilized migration as a political tool. Consequently, the analogy usually employed to depict migration streams, that of a constant ebb and flow, is of little use to describe the Cuban case. Rather, Cuban migration has been more akin to the flow from a water faucet: abruptly turned off and on at the will of those in power in Havana and Washington in response to political considerations. A climate of hostility and the absence of normal relations between the two countries, combined with the geographic fact that Cuba is an island, has made migration difficult and generally unavailable, except when the two governments, unilaterally or bilaterally, decide to provide the means for migration to occur. The timing, length, intensity, and characteristics of each wave are therefore largely a consequence of the conditions under which the migration from Cuba to the United States is allowed to take place. There have been four major and distinct migration waves to the United States from Cuba since the rise of the present Cuban government in 1959: (1) the early exiles, 1959–1962; (2) the "airlift" from 1965–1973; (3) Mariel (1980); and (4) the 1994 "rafters."

The Early Exiles, 1959–1962

The first wave amounted to about 200,000 persons (Pérez 1986a, 129). The U.S. government facilitated their entry by granting them refugee status, allowing them to enter without the restrictions imposed on most other nationality groups (Masud-Piloto 1988, 32–35). A program was established to assist in the resettlement and economic adjustment of the arrivals (Pedraza-Bailey 1985, 40–52).

In this initial wave, Cuba's displaced and alienated elite tended to predominate among the migrants. The contentious transition from capitalism to socialism affected first and foremost the upper sectors of Cuban society (Fagen, Brody, and O'Leary 1968, 19–22). Many of those estranged from the revolutionary process were also fearful of the implications of the changes for their children, especially with the nationalization of private schools. Consequently, families of upper socioeconomic status with children under eighteen years of age are over-represented in this wave. But as María Teresa Carrera's story above poignantly showed, as many as 14,000 children also arrived unaccompanied during this period.

The importance of this first wave in shaping the character of the Cuban presence in the United States cannot be overstated. As might be expected given its socioeconomic origins, this wave possessed skills and attitudes that would facilitate adjustment to life in the United States and give it an enduring political and economic hegemony within the Cuban American community (Portes and Stepick 1993, 123–149). Labeled the "Golden Exile," it is the wave that has been most economically successful (Portes 1969). Furthermore, those early migrants felt compelled into exile as they found themselves on the losing side of Cuba's internal class conflict. They have therefore been the principal standard-bearers in the sustained struggle against the Cuban government, the faithful keepers of the exile legacy.

The Airlift, 1965–1973

The second wave started in the fall of 1965 when the Cuban government opened a port and allowed persons from the United States to go to Cuba to pick up relatives who wanted to leave the country. Some 5,000 persons left from the port of Camarioca before the United States and Cuba halted the boatlift and agreed to an orderly airlift. The airlift, also called the "freedom flights," started in December 1965 and lasted until 1973. The twice-daily flights from Cuba to Miami brought 260,500 persons during those years, making it the largest of all the waves, although it was much less intense than the others, taking place over eight years (Pérez 1986a, 130).

The airlift allowed the Cuban government to pick and choose from a large pool of applicants for a departure permit. Males of military age were excluded and the government expedited the applications of the elderly. With a predominance of females and the elderly, airlift arrivals had a profile that was very different from the typical immigrant to the United States. In its first few years, the airlift brought the remnants of Cuba's upper classes, especially the elderly parents of those who had left in the earlier wave. But by the late 1960s, with the advent of sustained austerity in Cuba, the airlift started to peel away at the middle sectors of Cuba's social class structure: small entrepreneurs, skilled and semiskilled workers, and white-collar employees (Pedraza 1996, 267). By 1973, however, the applications for departure apparently bottomed-out and both governments agreed to terminate the airlift.

Mariel, 1980

By 1980, the pressure within Cuba for emigration rose once again. The number of unauthorized departures increased. On April 1, a group of six persons violently entered the Peruvian embassy in Havana seeking asylum, resulting in the death of one of the embassy's Cuban guards. The Cuban government withdrew all guards from the Peruvian compound, an action that caused the embassy to flood with more than 10,000 people seeking to leave the country. The Cuban government responded to the crisis by opening a port for unrestricted emigration. The port was Mariel, giving the name to a boatlift that brought, in a manner uncontrolled by the United States, more than 125,000 Cubans into the country. It was not as large as the previous waves, but it took place during only five months.

The Mariel exodus was a chaotic migration on vessels that went to Cuba from Florida to pick up relatives of persons already residing in the United States. More than just the relatives boarded the boats, however, and the result was a wave that is perhaps the closest to being representative of the Cuban population. It included, for the first time, sizable representation from Cuba's lower socioeconomic sectors and its nonwhite population. There were convicted felons among the arrivals, but there were also writers, artists, professionals, and even government officials.

The Mariel boatlift originated and unfolded in a dramatic fashion. The death of Ibis Guerrero's family was one of the most tragic episodes of that exodus, but by no means the only one. Thousands of

Mariel arrivals were interned in refugee camps in the United States until sponsors could be found for them. Those who were classified as criminals and therefore "excludable" from the United States were never released. Nearly 1,000 of them were eventually deported to Cuba under an agreement with the Cuban government (Lisandro Pérez 1999, 199).

Despite the negative press that the Mariel arrivals received in the United States, the traditional open-door U.S. policy towards Cubans continued during those five months in 1980. But it was clear, after the boatlift was finally halted, that the welcome mat that Americans had always been willing to extend to Cubans had worn thin.

The Rafter Crisis, 1994

Throughout the rest of the 1980s and the early 1990s there was a lull in migration from Cuba. Only about 2,000 persons were being admitted by the United States each year. The pressure for massive emigration rose once again, however, and during the first few months of 1994 there were a number of dramatic and violent incidents as Cubans seeking to leave crashed into embassies, commandeered planes, helicopters, and boats to the United States, and departed in makeshift rafts, or, in the case of Eugenio Maderal, on a surfboard. As happened in 1980, the unauthorized departures resulted in tragedy. When a Cuban government vessel attempted to stop a hijacked tugboat, more than forty of its occupants drowned, including children. Another hijacking resulted in the death of a Cuban police officer.

As in 1980, the Cuban government responded by reopening the faucet, announcing on August 11 that it would not detain anyone trying to leave Cuba in a raft or other vessel. As a result, nearly 37,000 Cubans were rescued by the U.S. Coast Guard in less than a month. The bulk of the arrivals, including Margarita Uría, were detained for more than a year in camps at the U.S. naval base in Guantánamo. Remembering the Mariel experience, the United States was unwilling this time to hold the door open for Cubans. President Clinton and his Attorney General placed the rescued rafters in Guantánamo with the expectation that they would never be admitted into the United States. The absence of alternative destinations for the rafters, as well as the deteriorating conditions in the camps, eventually prompted the United States to admit them into the country.

The rafter crisis of 1994 was halted after only one month when negotiations between the two countries resulted in an agreement whereby the United States committed to admit at least 20,000 Cubans a year through the normal visa process. For their part, the Cubans agreed to accept the return of any future unauthorized emigrants interdicted by the U.S. Coast Guard before reaching U.S. shores.

The rafter crisis, 1994. As soon as the Cuban government temporarily suspended intercepting unauthorized emigrants, Cubans constructed makeshift vessels and left the island in broad daylight. Here, a crowd of people from the coastal town of Cojímar watch a group depart in a raft made of inner tubes.

(The Miami Herald/Al Diaz)

CONCLUSION: CUBAN MIGRATION AT THE TURN OF THE CENTURY

With the end of the 1994 rafter crisis, one faucet had closed and another had opened. During the rest of the 1990s and into the twenty-first century, about 20,000 Cubans arrived each year through a legal and orderly process. Unauthorized migrations, however, persisted, although many no longer came in rickety rafts. The migration agreement forced those wishing to leave the country to not only elude the Cuban patrols, but also the U.S. Coast Guard. To be reasonably sure of reaching U.S. shores a powerboat was needed. The paid smuggler entered the picture, transporting human cargo across the Florida Strait at top speed under the cloak of night, ushering in yet another dramatic and bizarre chapter in the migration of Cubans to the United States.

At the close of the twentieth century, the U.S. Bureau of the Census estimated that there were about 1.2 million persons of Cuban "origin or descent" living in the United States. By far most of them, more than 700,000, were actually born in Cuba and arrived after the 1959 revolution. By century's end an overwhelming majority (nearly 65 percent) of all Cubans in the United States lived in southern Florida, and will probably continue to concentrate there well into the twenty-first century. Miami is the principal stage of the Cuban American community, where most of the recurring dramas of exile have taken place.

The twentieth century ended with the staging in Miami, and in Cuba, of a drama of unparalleled intensity. The saga of the child Elián González is a fitting conclusion to the Cuban American experience of the nineteenth and twentieth centuries. It is appropriate that the story that started with Varela end with Elián. No one has made more transparent than this child the recurring theme of the Cuban presence in the United States during two centuries: the power of political forces to sweep up and profoundly transform the courses of individual lives.

3

Culture

Exceptionalism, Diversity, and Secularism

In 1960, Jean-Paul Sartre, the French existentialist writer, visited Cuba. The legend goes that among his parting words as he boarded the plane for Paris was this assessment of Cuba: "one cannot live here...it is too surreal."

We do not know if he really did say those words, or if he did, why he reached such a conclusion, but they are an appropriate start to a discussion about Cuban culture. That culture has such a unique composition and diversity that it would not be surprising if an astute outside observer, existentialist or not, found it surreal.

Consider the following statements comparing the history and culture of Cuba with those of its neighbors in this hemisphere:

1. Cuba is perhaps the only country of Latin America in which the impact of its aboriginal cultures is viewed as insignificant and has been virtually erased from the national consciousness.

2. Cuba is the most "Spanish" country of Latin America.

3. Cuba is the most "African" country of Spanish America.

4. Cuba was the Latin American country first and most profoundly affected by the spread of U.S. economic, political, social, and cultural institutions and influences before and during the twentieth century.

5. During the past four decades, Cuba has been isolated from most its neighbors; it has a political and economic system creatively borrowed from the Soviet Union, Eastern Europe, and China; it is the only country in the hemisphere presumably guided by socialist principles; it is the only Latin American country that has undertaken a large military campaign outside the hemisphere (and in Africa, at that).

Even if some of the statements above are arguable, the fact that one can seriously apply all five to one country, an island with barely

11 million people, gives some idea of the extraordinary and conflicting forces that have shaped Cuban culture. It is a unique combination that has created a diverse, contradictory, and enigmatic culture that may indeed appear surreal to many.

If we focus on the area that is of greatest interest here, the culture of Cubans in the United States, we have to add yet another statement to the five above: a massive and largely selective emigration has spanned four decades, occurring within a highly politicized climate of hostility and creating a large community of exiles in opposition to, and largely isolated from, the home country. We can only wonder at what Sartre might have said had he visited Miami. The circumstances inherent in the exile condition can have a distorting effect on the culture the exiles take to their new home. If, to begin with, that culture of the home country is fraught with contradictions and complexities, then the possibility of grasping, much less explaining, the culture of the émigrés becomes a daunting task.

This chapter focuses primarily on three major themes that have been dominant in Cuban culture: exceptionalism, diversity, and secularism. Despite the intricacies of Cuban culture, these are constant and identifiable tendencies, deeply rooted in Cuban history, which have clear and consequential manifestations in the culture of Cubans in the United States.

EXCEPTIONALISM

All peoples believe that their culture is unique, unlike any other. It is part of the ethnocentrism that is found, to a greater or lesser degree, in all cultures. With Cubans, however, that sense of uniqueness is elevated to the point where it is a defining national characteristic, a part of the national consciousness that influences the perception of the place of Cuba, and Cubans, in the world and its relations with its neighbors. It is what can be called a culture of exceptionalism, a shared perception that the national experience has been different from that of any other people. This sense of uniqueness has frequently led Cubans to proudly set themselves apart from other cultures. This was true among the *habaneros* of the nineteenth century who perceived that they occupied a privileged position within the Spanish empire, quite distinct from that of the rest Spanish America and the Caribbean. This is also true among contemporary Cubans in Miami who believe that their experience is quite different from that of other Latino immigrants, defying efforts to be placed under the same panethnic label.

In the case of Cubans, ethnocentrism and a culture of exceptionalism have been reinforced by objective historical reality. The fact is that nineteenth century *habaneros* did occupy a unique position within the

Spanish empire, and Cubans in Miami have had a qualitatively different experience from that of other Latino immigrants. Cuban exceptionalism has historical roots.

The origins of Cuban exceptionalism can be found almost at the very outset of the Spanish colonization of the island and are linked to a critical factor in Cuban colonial history: location. Location played a fundamental role in shaping Cuba's development within the Spanish empire. Once the Spanish were unable to find in Cuba the mineral riches they were seeking, they moved on to the mainland of North and South America, where they did find ample supplies of precious ores. Throughout most of the sixteenth century, Cuba became virtually depopulated as the sparse aboriginal population was decimated and the Spanish had little interest in settling Cuba. The treasures in gold and silver found among the aboriginal civilizations of Mexico, Central, and South America had to be shipped home through waters that were becoming increasingly infested with foreign pirates eager to lighten the loads of the Spanish galleons. A convoy system was thus established by which the ships leaving the two principal mainland ports, Veracruz and Cartagena de Indias, would meet in a Caribbean port and then proceed together, escorted by warships, across the Atlantic. It was called the *flota* system. The logical location for that pivotal Caribbean port would have been the oldest Spanish harbor settlement in the New World: Santo Domingo. But that would have required the ships to sail through the dangerous southern Caribbean Sea on their way to the Atlantic. Furthermore, the Spanish discovered the Gulf Stream, a current that passes through the Straits of Florida and greatly facilitates sailing by literally pushing ships out to the Atlantic. Four centuries later, that same current would help Cuban rafters get to the United States clandestinely.

The route through the Gulf of Mexico and the Straits of Florida favored the settlement and development of an excellent harbor that was located in just the right place: the northwestern coast of Cuba. It was a large, deep, and well-protected harbor, with a narrow entrance that facilitated its defense. In 1514, the city of San Cristóbal de La Habana was established on that harbor. For centuries after that, Havana would be the pivotal axis for virtually all travel and trade between Spain and its colonies in the Caribbean and the Circum-Caribbean. Havana became the crossroads of the Spanish empire and the English colonies of North America and the Caribbean. The most prominent feature of the Cuban national seal is a key, recognizing the historical role of the island as "the key to the Americas." It is not surprising that Havana was always a city with an international orientation. Walled off from its sparsely-settled hinterland, the thriving city faced only the harbor, and through it, the world, which came knocking at its doorstep. When the British decided to strike at the Spanish empire

Havana's importance. In colonial times, all principal Spanish trade routes in the Circum Caribbean led to and from Cuba's capital.

in the New World during the Thirty Years' War, there was really only one desirable strategic target: Havana, which they occupied for eleven months in 1762. That occupation would establish permanent economic, cultural, and social ties between *habaneros* and the English colonies of North America.

Those ties to the north would be strengthened as the Spanish empire waned in the nineteenth century. When the United States acquired Cuba through the war against Spain in 1898, it ruled the island until 1902, and again from 1906 to 1909. Throughout the first half of the twentieth century, U.S. economic, political, social, and cultural influence on the island was pervasive (Louis A. Pérez, Jr. 1999). Havana continued its role as a pivotal city for a superpower. Through Havana to the rest of the island flowed the investments, goods, and sociocultural influences that inextricably tied Cuba to its powerful northern neighbor. Nowhere in Latin America did the United States have such an early and predominant presence as in Cuba. By the middle of the twentieth century, Cuba was at the cutting edge of the modernizing in-

The busy port of Havana in the mid-nineteenth century. Since the city's founding, the port has been the its principal function, primarily because of location, the large and secure bay (on the left), and the narrow and defensible passage to the ocean (on the right).

Engraving by Eduardo Laplante (1818–?), reproduced in Pintura española y cubana y litografías y grabados cubanos del siglo XIX *(Colección del Museo Nacional de La Habana), Ministerio de Cultura, Dirección de Bellas Artes y Archivos, Madrid, 1983, p. 98.*

fluence that had spread from the United States to the rest of the hemisphere. The island, and especially its capital city, was awash in the culture, technology, and consumer goods that poured in from the most powerful country in the world, located only ninety miles away. As in colonial times, the Cubans had every reason to believe they occupied a unique and privileged position in the world order, reinforcing a sense of singularity and self-importance in relation to its Latin American and Caribbean neighbors.

That pervasive U.S. influence was dramatically replaced, starting in 1959, with a political and economic system that, in a different way, would push to new heights the Cubans' sense of exceptionalism. The establishment, in the thick of the Cold War, of a centrally planned economic system closely allied with the Soviet bloc, and consequent hostile relations with the United States, was an unforseen and unprecedented model for a Latin American nation to follow. That such a model was adopted at the doorstep of the United States had the consequence of placing Cuba near the center of superpower confrontations, giving it a far greater role and visibility in international matters than what a Caribbean island could be expected to assume. The greatest debacle of the Kennedy administration was the Bay of Pigs. The closest the world has come to nuclear war (in October 1962) was over

Cuba. Not content to be a mere pawn in the conflict between superpowers, Cuba deployed tens of thousands of troops in Africa in the 1970s, defeating the South Africans in a critical battle and becoming an important player in the political resolution of the status of Namibia. To this day, Cuba is an exception, not only in the hemisphere, but in the world, as its leadership tries to defy the trend towards globalization and insists on keeping Cuba as one of only a handful of nations regarding themselves as "socialist." Singular prominence in the political arena has also been accompanied by results in competitive sports. Few countries as small as Cuba, both demographically and economically, can come even close to claiming the success that Cuba has had over the past three decades in international competitions, especially the Olympics.

Even Cuba's emigration is marked by exceptionalism. As we saw in Chapter 2, the revolution produced an exodus with a singular history. Based initially on the displacement of its elite, that emigration has maintained an exile ethos, created a powerful ethnic enclave, and exhibits relatively high levels of economic and political influence at both the local and national levels. Any overview of U.S. immigration or of the Latino population is likely to note that the Cuban experience has been different, that Cubans represent a distinct group that should be viewed separately. That distinctness is highly valued by many Cubans, who have long maintained that they are "exiles" who felt compelled to leave the island for political reasons, unlike most other "immigrants" who came to this country for economic reasons.

In summary: throughout their history, in Cuba as well as outside the island, Cubans have had ample reasons to develop a sense of exceptionalism. It has been a perennial national cultural trait, with mixed consequences. Exceptionalism has contributed to a very strong sense of national identity—an unshakeable shared identification with their national place of origin. Indeed, Cubans thought of themselves as Cubans for at least two centuries before the creation of a Cuban nation-state. In the United States, Cubans exhibit a strong tendency to resist being culturally assimilated into non-Cuban categories, especially pan-ethnic labels. As one bumper sticker in Miami reads: *Yo no soy hispano...yo soy cubano* (I am not Hispanic...I am Cuban).

The downside of exceptionalism is insularity and separateness. One of the many reasons José Martí has always been considered an extraordinary Cuban (even by Cubans themselves) is that he had an odd trait for a Cuban: a well-developed sense of panamericanism. One of the pervasive themes of his writings was to define Cuba, and himself as a Cuban, as part of the hemisphere and to tie Cuba to the history and culture of its neighbors. Most of his compatriots, accustomed to looking at themselves as distinct and conditioned by history to turning their attention outward from the Caribbean, first to Spain, and then to the north, have not generally shared that vision. The absence of a pan-american vision is a factor that affects relations between Cubans and other Latinos in the United States. It is a trait that has reinforced the insularity of the Miami enclave, discussed in Chapter 4.

DIVERSITY

It is not surprising that a Cuban anthropologist was one of the first intellectual voices of the twentieth century to challenge the adequacy of the concept of "acculturation." Viewing it as a "process of transfer from one culture to another," Fernando Ortiz found acculturation to be an inappropriate term to describe the development of Cuban culture. Instead, he coined, in 1940, a term he called "transculturation," which he felt better described the entirety of the process of cultural change and development that occurred in Cuba as a result of the constant contact of peoples with different cultural origins. Acquiring new cultural traits, acculturation, is only the beginning. The cultures in contact also lose part of their cultures, and eventually there is the creation of a new culture, with traits from the original cultures, but distinct from them.

> We have selected the term *transculturation* to express the extremely varied phenomena that originate in Cuba through the very complex transmutations of culture that take place here, without which it is impossible to understand the evolution of the Cuban people…the true history of Cuba is the history of its very intricate transculturations. (Ortiz 1940, 99)

Ortiz spent most of his long and productive scholarly career studying those "intricate transculturations" in an effort to understand Cuban culture. It is a big task. Cuba's location and its role as a crossroads made contact between cultures a constant throughout its history—not just a modern phenomenon derived from the increase in voluntary migration and the improvements in transportation. Even in precolumbian times, more than one indigenous culture coexisted on the island. Ortiz was engaged in the questions: What culture? Whose culture?

The Spanish, of course, are viewed as the principal contributors to the development of Cuban culture. But Ortiz used the concept of transculturation to show that even before the twentieth century, Cuban culture had ceased to be "Spanish" and had become something new, something Cuban, a result of all those intricate transculturations. His major contribution was to show that in that transculturation process, the influence of African culture cannot be underestimated, and certainly not ignored, as had been done by many Cuban scholars before him.

The Spanish and African cultures have weighed in so heavily in the process of shaping Cuban culture that it is possible to state, as was done at the outset of this chapter, that Cuba's culture is the most

"Spanish" of all in Latin America, and at the same time the most "African" of Spanish America. This is perhaps the most intriguing (or surreal) paradox of Cuban culture.

The Spanish

It is not difficult to trace the reasons for the extraordinary influence of Spain on Cuban culture. The Spanish colonized an island with an indigenous population that was relatively small and which virtually disappeared soon after colonization. The Iberian colonizers ruled the island during four centuries. The *flota* system, as already described, established a special direct relationship between Spain and Cuba, as Havana became the point of contact between Madrid and most of its New World colonies. While the bulk of those colonies gained their independence in the early nineteenth century, Cuba remained in the Spanish empire almost into the twentieth century, becoming the jewel of the Spanish crown. It is estimated that during the last three decades of the nineteenth century, one million Spaniards migrated to Cuba. More than half were soldiers under orders not to lose the jewel (Moreno Fraginals 1995, 296).

Even when the protracted struggle for independence broke out in 1868 and continued for three decades, the conflict was over national sovereignty and self-determination. Spain was never viewed as representing a foreign culture. There was therefore no trace of a cultural conflict or of a rejection of the culture of the colonial power in the independence movement. The writings of José Martí, a leader of that movement, are devoid of any repudiation or hate of the Spanish and their culture. Martí himself was the son of a Spanish military man deployed to Cuba.

The end of Spanish rule in Cuba did not sever ties between the two countries. When the United States acquired the island from Spain in 1898, it sought to maintain existing property rights. Consequently, the Spanish were never divested of their businesses and property in Cuba, nor were they expelled, as often happens when a colony is lost. The Spanish largely retained their physical and economic presence in Cuba into the twentieth century. Not just property holders and other civilians remained in Cuba, but also many Spanish soldiers who refused to be shipped back to Spain and retired (or even deserted) from the military and stayed on the island (Moreno Fraginals 1995, 296). A census taken by the United States one year after acquiring Cuba found some 130,000 Spanish-born persons living in the island, representing nearly nine percent of the total population (U.S. War Department 1900, 218). Even that figure is considered a gross undercount since many Spaniards may have been hesitant to identify themselves as Spanish-born in a census administered by the United States.

The continued demographic and economic Spanish presence in Cuba, coupled with prosperity during the initial decades of the twentieth century, produced a massive new wave of Spanish migration to the island. A 1919 census found more than 245,000 Spanish-born persons living in Cuba (Census National Board of Cuba 1920, 432).

By mid-century Cuba still retained the indelible mark of Spanish culture. It is an influence that has been maintained by Cubans in the United States, as those who left Cuba after 1959 were drawn from the sectors of Cuban society most intensively shaped by Spanish culture: the entrepreneurial middle and upper, white, and urban sectors. Many Cubans in the United States are second or third generation Spaniards. Spain is without a doubt the leading tourist destination for Cuban Americans. Miami boasts by far the largest number of Spanish restaurants of any city in the United States (most with flamenco floor shows) and the largest number of shops selling Spanish imports (especially food). Several private dance schools in Miami, run by Cubans, teach traditional Spanish dance forms to young Cuban Americans. Whereas many Latino groups in the United States, especially Mexicans, keep Spain and its culture at arm's length, reflecting an awareness of its history as a ruthless colonizer of indigenous Americans, Cubans explicitly recognize and embrace the Spanish legacy in their culture.

The Africans

Music, art, religion, food and diet, idioms and jargon, norms and values: is there any aspect of Cuban culture that does not show the influence of the cultures the African slaves took with them to Cuba? Many observers of modern Cuba, Ortiz foremost among them, have noted the vitality and evident presence of African cultural traits in the island's culture. In few countries of Latin America has the process of transculturation produced a culture that so clearly manifests its African lineage. The explanation lies in the size and timing of the arrival waves of Africans to Cuba. Nowhere in Spanish America did Africans arrive as massively so late in the colonial era.

Africans started arriving in Cuba not long after the Spanish. But it was not until the late eighteenth century that the importation of African slaves took on massive proportions. Until that time, the soil of Cuba was not intensively cultivated nor was the island densely settled. Aside from Havana, the Spanish had little interest in Cuba. There were large cattle ranches and also modest plantations of sugar, tobacco, and coffee with fairly small slave populations. In 1774, after nearly three centuries of colonial rule, the entire island had only 172,000 inhabitants, and about half lived in Havana. Slaves represented less than one-fourth of the population.

What changed all that and brought a dramatic transformation to Cuba was the sugar revolution that started in the late eighteenth century and lasted until the middle of the nineteenth. It was the most significant economic and social phenomenon of colonial Cuba. The island's economy was radically transformed as small agricultural producers were virtually eliminated in western Cuba and a new class of wealthy native-born *habaneros* started producing sugar on a large scale (Moreno Fraginals 1978). The small sugar mills, with limited land and relatively few slaves, gave way to huge landholdings where sugar cane was processed in larger, technically advanced mills. Those mills required more sugar cane, hence more land, and, of course, more labor, resulting in the massive importation of African slaves. By 1841 the population of the island had multiplied and passed the one million mark. Slaves accounted for 44 percent (Knight 1970, 22). No other sugar-producing colony of the New World experienced such a massive entry of Africans in the nineteenth century.

Aside from the sheer volume of the African arrivals, the manner in which the slaves were introduced conditioned their subsequent impact on Cuban culture. During the sugar revolution there was no longer the pretense in Cuba that slavery served to "civilize" the heathen and that owners had the responsibility of evangelizing their slaves. In this new system of mass production, the slave became a resource to be exploited, seven days a week for as many hours daily as the slave could bear. At night, the slaves were locked into crowded and stifling dormitories. The chapel and the priest disappeared from the mills as the slaveowners refused to provide the necessary economic support. Gone were the paternalistic efforts to "civilize" slaves, to Christianize them, to give them time for mass and the sacraments, to teach them Spanish. In other words, there was no interest in the "acculturation" of the Africans. This made possible the continued vitality of many elements of African culture.

By the end of the slave trade late in the nineteenth century, there were hundreds of thousands of first and second generation Africans in Cuba among whom African cultural influences remained strong. The impact of this on the transculturation process that led to the creation of the modern culture of Cuba cannot be underestimated. The best example is the music that Cubans created during the first half of the twentieth century, a result of the mixture of African and European elements and instrumentation.

Among Cubans in the United States, the impact of African culture is somewhat more muted in comparison with the culture in the island. The socioeconomic selectivity of the migration drew disproportionately from the "whiter" sectors of Cuban society. More than 90 percent of Cubans in the United States consistently identify as "white" in the decennial censuses. In contrast, it is estimated that at least half, if not more, of the island's population has some degree of African ancestry. But even if somewhat muted, the African contribution is undeniably present among Cubans in the United States, if only because it has become part of the culture that the exiles strive hard to maintain in the United States. In music, food and diet, art, and idioms, the culture of Cubans in the United States carries the marks of the African legacy in the country of origin.

Direct reminders of Cuba's African heritage can be found in the countless establishments throughout Miami, called *botánicas*, which sell the goods and paraphernalia associated with the practices of Afro-Cuban religious cults. The distinctions between Catholicism and the beliefs of African origin are not always clear, since a considerable amount of transculturation has occurred between the two. A number of Catholic saints, for example, are especially important in the religious practices of Cubans who consider themselves Catholic, yet the prominence of those particular saints stems from their identification with deities, or *orishas*, in the pantheon of the Yoruba, one of the African ethnic groups most common among slaves in Cuba.

As with all folk religions, the Afro-Cuban cults have a tremendous resiliency and appeal because the belief systems address the everyday problems people face in health, romance, survival, prosperity, and other personal issues. Many of the rituals hold the promise of resolving problems in these areas, and therefore hold special appeal for immigrants facing an unfamiliar world and uncertain future.

Traditionally, there has been a relationship between the practice of Afro-Cuban religions and socioeconomic status. In general, the presence of evident African cultural influences in music, diet, and even diction, has long been associated with lower socioeconomic status in Cuba.

Since the upper socioeconomic groups were overrepresented in the early wave of migration from Cuba, Afro-Cuban religious practices were not much in evidence among Cubans in Miami prior to 1965. As successive migrant waves became more representative of the Cuban population, the Afro-Cuban cults made greater inroads in U.S. Cuban communities. The Mariel boatlift was especially important in increasing the number of practitioners in the various Afro-Cuban cults.

Other Influences

Despite the predominance of the Spanish/African mix, the Cuban cultural landscape would not be so "intricate" (as Ortiz viewed it) if it did not have greater complexity. The "key to the Americas" received people from many other cultures who left an indelible mark on the transculturation process.

Foremost among them were the Chinese, who came in two waves. The first was in the mid-nineteenth century when Chinese arrived as "coolies" under labor contracts, to supplement the African workforce in agriculture. In 1877 more than 40,000 Chinese-born persons lived in Cuba, 99.8 percent of them males. The second wave came during the initial decades of the twentieth century. Most of these Chinese newcomers engaged in small-scale entrepreneurship in Cuba's large cities (Guanche 1996, 84–87). By mid-century, Havana boasted one of the largest Chinatowns in Latin America. Because it was an exclusively male migration, Chinese immigrants tended to marry outside the group, especially nonwhite women (Baltar Rodríguez 1997, 89–90).

Given the importance of business ownership among Chinese Cubans, many chose to leave the island after 1959. Many relocated to New York and eventually to Miami. One of the most visible signs of their presence in the United States is the "Chinese Cuban" restaurant, serving a unique combination of Chinese and Cuban dishes, of which pork fried rice with a side of fried plantains is the most common.

Many other cultures have contributed to the intricacies of Cuban culture, mostly as a result of migration to the island during the first half of the twentieth century. West Indians (especially Jamaicans and Haitians) went to eastern Cuba to cut sugarcane. Many were repatriated in the 1930s when there was no longer a labor shortage (Guanche 1996, 96). Eastern European Jews came to represent a numerous and visible community, especially in Havana, and later, in Miami (Levine 1993 and Bettinger-López 2000). Other groups came from the Middle East and even the United States. In 1931, 11 percent of the Cuban population was foreign-born. An even larger percentage were children of immigrants.

To this complex mix must be added the pervasive influence of U.S. culture that we noted earlier. By the time the exodus from Cuba to the United States started in 1960, Cuban culture was an extremely diverse and elaborate mosaic. It is that culture that then underwent a further process of transculturation in the United States as Cubans adapted to life there. That adaptation process has been different within the Miami enclave than elsewhere in the United States. It was also different for the initial cohort of exiles than for Mariel entrants and for the rafters. We are left with a diverse and intricate picture that defies generalizations regarding the "culture" of Cubans in the United States.

SECULARISM

In August of 1880, after eight months on the job, Havana's Spanish-born bishop, Ramón Fernández Piérola y López de Luzuriaga, wrote a letter to a colleague back home in which he expressed this forlorn conclusion about Cuba:

> I have come to believe that in this country there has never been a religious base; that is to say, that we Spanish have not been fortunate, for that which characterizes us and which we have taken everywhere, religion, we did not bring here. (Maza Miquel 1990, 12)

More than half a century later, another foreign observer, the Dominican Juan Bosch, argued that the Catholic Church "abstained from deforming the Cuban soul with fanaticisms and persecutions, so that hedonism has taken possession of the Cubans" (Bosch 1955, 203).

From the earliest colonial times to the present, the secular character of Cuban society has been repeatedly noted by many observers. Perhaps no explanation for this phenomenon is more important than the historical conditions discussed earlier: Cuba's location, its role in the Spanish empire, and Havana's primacy as a port city. The major Spanish settlements in the Americas were typically established in inland and remote locations on or near Indian settlements. That relative isolation contributed to the firm establishment of the Catholic Church and religiosity, from the very founding of those settlements.

In contrast, Havana was a crossroads and developed all the characteristics usually associated with busy port cities:

> Havana early acquired a tawdry appearance and became a city teeming with merchants, vendors, gamblers, deserters, and peddlers...many passengers arrived weighed down with fortunes made on the mainland, and relieving them of this weight engaged the resourcefulness of *habaneros* of all sectors of society. Lodging and dining facilities increased... retail trade expanded. So too did illicit trade and commercialized vice. Brothels early established something of a ubiquitous presence in Havana. (Pérez 1988, 37)

Throughout the early colonial period, clerics worried and complained about the "immorality of Havana," with so many "mariners and transients" (Maza Miquel 1990, 2–3). One historian has described Havana as "unique, easy-going, brilliant but semi-criminal, maritime and cosmopolitan" (Thomas 1971, 12).

The unquestionably secular character of Havana permeated Cuban society. Throughout most the colonial era, this "immoral" city contained more than half of the population of the entire island. Cuba's distinct urban character had as its flip side the abandonment of the countryside. If Spain paid little attention to the development of Cuba, other than as a crossroads of the fleet, so did the Catholic

Church. The island was perennially understaffed by the Church, and the priests were concentrated in cities, especially Havana. In comparison with the riches of the Church elsewhere in the Spanish empire, the Cuban Church was poor in resources. No Cuban cathedral, for example, has ever rivaled those built in the principal cities of Spanish America. The presence of the Catholic Church in Cuba was much weaker than almost anywhere else in Latin America.

The secularism of Cuban society was reinforced by the economic, social, and cultural influence of the United States and, of course, the subsequent Marxist ideological character of the Cuban Revolution. In Chapter 5 we discuss the overwhelming trend toward modernity and secularism in the family-related norms and legislation during the Cuban Republic. The migration to the United States drew primarily from the most modernized and urban sectors of twentieth century Cuban society.

Secularism is an important key to understanding the culture of Cubans in the United States. In fact, if one were to make a list of the ten most prominent voluntary associations among Cubans in the United States, it is not likely that even one would be religiously based. Instead, they would be either civic and professional organizations or "exile" organizations concerned with the "recovery" of the homeland (political, nostalgic, militant, etc.).

Among Cubans, secularism has a clear corollary: a virtual absence of fatalism, a cultural value that has been traditionally widespread in Latin America. Cubans are confident they can control their destiny, that their lives are in their own hands. This is an important trait related to the rise of entrepreneurship. Also, the historical importance of Havana as a trade center created opportunities for making a living from buying and selling, very early placing a value on business ownership. Throughout Cuba's history the influx of commerce and capital, from Spain or from the United States, generated the conditions for social mobility through entrepreneurship. Fidel Castro once derisively referred to this trait when he listed the barriers to the creation of a socialist economy: "We are a nation with a shopkeeper mentality."

The establishment of a socialist economy led to the emigration of many with just such a "shopkeeper mentality." As will be seen in the next chapter, entrepreneurship is at the heart of the creation of the enclave. In their own version of the Weberian notion that a value system supported the rise of capitalism, Cubans in the United States have placed a value on business ownership as a vehicle for upward mobility and for shaping one's destiny. Secularism and the absence of fatalism, values honed by a centuries-old commercial port culture, are at the heart of the entrepreneurial character of Cuban Miami.

CONCLUSION

Music, Cuba's most notable contribution to world culture, provides a fitting subject with which to summarize the themes explored in this chapter: exceptionalism, diversity, and secularism in Cuban and Cuban American culture.

The music of Cuba is the product of a society shaped by an extraordinary set of circumstances. Its exceptional quality is rooted in the diverse elements that came together to produce something new, but that still reflect their different lineages. There are *rhumba* and *comparsa* compositions, for example, that fuse Spanish melodies and instrumentations with African percussion and feature a Chinese "cornet." The core of the Cuban sound is the intricate overlaying of various rhythm lines within a single tempo. The result is a myriad of complex music forms that defy neat categorizations.

Cuban music is a distinctly secular music, even more, a sensual music, very much of this world. It is the music of love, seduction, dancing; music for the nightclub, the smoke-filled bar, the jamsession, the *carnaval*. It is not the music of the church choir, the altar, or the divine. It is the music of an "immoral" port culture perennially at a crossroads. In a recent compilation of the "100 Cuban Songs of the Millenium" by a noted Cuban musicologist, not one of those 100 songs can be even remotely characterized as religious.

The music produced by Cubans in the United States is deeply rooted in the Cuban tradition, but it has undergone its own unavoidable process of transculturation in this country. The so-called "Miami Sound," for example, is, above anything else, Cuban music, but it shows a clear influence of 60s' rock, not to mention the fact that the lyrics are sometimes in English.

Obviously, music is not the only area of the culture of Cuban Americans that in the process of migration underwent, and is undergoing, the "very intricate transculturations" that Ortiz argued have been the hallmarks of the development of Cuban culture. In that sense, the culture of Cubans in the United States has continued the historical process that started in the island centuries ago. But having evolved during at least the past four decades in a different context and with limited contact with the homeland, the culture of Cuban Americans has undoubtedly developed traits and patterns that differ from the culture of Cubans living now in the island.

Despite those expected differences, it is clear from this chapter that the major historical tendencies of Cuban culture—exceptionalism, diversity, and secularism—continue to permeate the lives of Cuban Americans.

4

iami

This Land Is Our Land

What they gave me was a desk and a test, and they told me that the test would cost me 20 or 25 dollars. I paid the 20 or 25 dollars, but did not pass the test because number one: I did not read English, I had problems with the language; and number two, the type of test they can give you…are so that one will not pass it. Three weeks after…there were ads in the newspapers…looking for people. I returned. They gave me a little better attention this time, did not give me the test, but they did not let me in, either. I got in on the third time because my [Anglo] father-in-law was a member of a local and had become a friend of the local representative. I came in recommended by him and the business agent helped me pass the test and I started working.

Pepe, a Cuban immigrant

This is not the type of tale you expect to hear from a Cuban in Miami. Pepe's story goes against many of the stereotypes of Cubans in Miami: successful, rich, or at least middle class, and to the right of most conservatives. He is a carpenter by trade and a labor leader by conviction and his story is one of discrimination. He received a rough reception when he arrived from Cuba in 1961 ready to work in the United States. He didn't bring over any negative views about unions. Instead, he considered unions to be benevolent organizations designed to help workers in their times of need. His rejection by the Carpenters Union surprised but did not defeat him.

Pepe was excluded as a Cuban and had to rely on the power of an Anglo to get into the union. Eventually he was included, just as many other Cubans in Miami have managed to be included in organizations from banks to universities. As Pepe rose through the ranks, he remembered his first experience. Once in a position of power, Pepe proceeded to use it on behalf of those who had been victims of discrimination. Pepe began to rebuild the union by bringing in newcomers from all over Latin America. "The way that I see it, it is my job to give Hispanics a chance. If you are no good, you won't stay long but I will always give a Hispanic a chance to prove himself." Pepe eventually became President of the Carpenters Union Local and today is one of the four regional representatives of the United Brotherhood of Carpenters and Joiners International Union. The highest-ranking Latino in the union, he is responsible for the entire southeastern United States.

Pepe's story is not that atypical and that is why it is important. What is interesting about his experience for us is the process. Pepe, like other Cubans, arrived with skills and the need to use them. Many have met some resistance but eventually managed to work their way into organizations at a variety of levels. When given the chance to shape those organizations, Cubans exhibited a preference for other Cubans or Latin Americans. Multiply Pepe's tale thousands of times and you'll get a good idea of how Cubans have reshaped Miami since 1959 and how the Cuban enclave developed.

"WE MADE MIAMI"

When the Cuban Revolution triumphed in 1959, Miami won the "who gets the exiles" lottery. Few could have imagined that the first rush of exiles into South Florida represented the edges of a hurricane-force wave of immigration that would reshape the cultural, political, economic, and social contours of the sleepy tourist town called Miami. So it is not just ethnic bravado that makes Miami Cubans commonly assert that they have "made Miami what it is today" through their hard work and "Cuban ingenuity." There is considerable empirical evidence to support the assertion. Indeed, Miami is the only U.S. city where Hispanic immigrants have managed to create a successful and self-sustained ethnic economy in which the primary problems are not unemployment and welfare, but sources of capital and expanding markets.

The initial wave of Cubans coming into the United States after the Cuban Revolution arrived at the ideal time. The Civil Rights Movement had begun to make minority rights a reality and the 1964 Civil Rights Act would soon become law. The Cubans arrived as a tailor-made minority: white, skilled, and, so all thought, temporary. The fact that they were fleeing communism at the height of the Cold War increased their value as well.

Even economic forces seemed to favor the Cuban immigrants. The decades of the 1950s and 1960s comprised the apex of the most vigorous economic expansion in U.S. history: the post-war boom. The sunbelt, and Florida in particular, stood poised to benefit from globalization forces which would, within a decade, redistribute jobs and people from the northern industrial complex to the emerging service sector driven economy. The Cubans, settling in a quintessential sunbelt service sector city on the frontier with Latin America, made the most of their bilingual and geographic advantages to lead Miami into the post-industrial era. The script couldn't have been better as Cubans began to reinvent Miami in their own image.

Since the Cubans began settling in Miami, the city has become the most Latin of all U.S. cities. As the southernmost metropolis in the continental United States, lying almost due east from Mexico City, it is much closer to Havana, Cuba, and San Juan, Puerto Rico, than to any major U.S. city. It has been called the capital of the Caribbean. It has a higher proportion of foreign-born residents, most of whom are Latin, than any other major U.S. urban area. Elites from throughout the Caribbean maintain houses and bank accounts in Miami. Its community college has more foreign students, again primarily Latin, than any other college or university in the nation.

Undoubtedly the Cuban presence has increased the Latin American and Caribbean nature of Miami. Before 1960, Miami was a thoroughly American city, a southern American city firmly focused northward. Miami's population consisted largely of Black and White southern in-migrants and their descendants, transplanted northerners, including many Jews, and Bahamian and other Caribbean Blacks and their descendants. Starting in the 1920s the permanent resident population was supplemented by a large transient population of tourists and retirees from the Northeast and Midwest. Economically, Miami subsisted primarily by providing services to those who came from the North, the legendary "snowbirds" who flocked there to escape the inhospitable winters of the north.

Today, persons born in Cuba or of Cuban descent represent Miami's largest ethnic group. During the 1960s their concentrated settlement pattern gave the name of Little Havana to a portion of 8th Street near downtown Miami. By the start of the twenty-first century, however, they could be found in great numbers throughout most of Greater Miami.

The demographic importance of the Cuban presence in Miami is evident in myriad ways. The "Cubanness" of the city is manifested not only in demonstrable terms, such as economic activities and cultural events, but also in a more intangible manner, such as "ambience." From the sidewalk cafés in Little Havana serving high-octane Cuban coffee to the suburban grocery stores where Spanish-language brand names of exotic products fill the aisles, Cubans and their culture set the pace. David Rieff, a New Yorker who has written on Miami, has noted that Cubans have largely taken control of the "atmosphere" of the city. Today, Cubans have a sense of "rootedness" in Miami. Miami is the capital and mecca of U.S. Cubans. As Rieff (1987, 193) expressed it, "Cubans are probably the only people who really do feel comfortable in Dade County these days.... Miami is their town now."

Cubans feel this way, too. Those who lived in other parts of the United States before settling in Miami often came looking for the feel of "home." Rene Jose Silva, who moved to the United States at the age of five and was raised in Pennsylvania and New Jersey, spoke about what moving to Miami meant to him.

> "For me, living in Miami as a Cuban is very comfortable. It's very important for me to live here. I felt like a fish out of water for many years up in the north.... I feel at home here. This is the second largest Cuban city in the world after Havana and you can literally live here and not speak English if you like. So, you know, it's a very comfortable situation for me. I've been here now almost nine years and I wouldn't want to live anywhere except in a free Cuba, anywhere else, so. I think that kinda says it all about what Miami is for me." (Geldof 1991, 267)

Why do Cubans feel so at home in Miami? How can a group of immigrants call an entire metropolitan area, not just a neighborhood, their creation and their home? In the remainder of the chapter, we discuss how Cubans have managed to do this, with a focus on the dynamics of the "Cuban success story." We describe the social and economic structure of the Cuban community, and then argue that its relative success is based on three forms of capital—social, economic, and political—that have produced an extraordinary solidarity among Cubans in Miami.

"MIAMI MADE US:" CUBAN ECONOMIC SUCCESS

Crossing the Florida Straits has never been easy for Cubans. Many who came in the 1960s lost all of their possessions in the revolution or had to leave them behind when they left the country. Those who had been active in the anti-Castro movement were often traumatized by the killing or imprisonment of a loved one. Arriving in a strange land, usually penniless, almost always ignorant of the language, it was hardly a foregone conclusion that in one generation Cubans would achieve the kind of success and power that few if any immigrant communities in U.S. history attained in so short a time. But Cubans did achieve that success, and that should be regarded as an important accomplishment. Yet, for all their pain and uprooting,

Cubans have enjoyed clear advantages when compared with other immigrant groups, and they possessed a number of significant traits that contributed to their eventual success.

Miami's Cuban community is regarded as the foremost example in the United States of a true ethnic enclave. An ethnic enclave is "a distinctive economic formation, characterized by the spatial concentration of immigrants who organize a variety of enterprises to serve their own ethnic market and the general population" (Portes and Bach 1985, 203). The foundation of the enclave is not simply its size or scale, but its highly differentiated nature. The sheer numbers, nonetheless, are impressive. By the beginning of the 1990s, 42 percent of all enterprises in Miami-Dade County were Hispanic-owned, and the absolute number of Hispanic-owned business in the area was second only to Los Angeles, which has a much larger Hispanic population. However, Hispanic businesses in Miami on average generate far more revenue than their counterparts in California (Metro-Dade County 1993). Three-quarters of Hispanic-owned enterprises in Miami are controlled by Cubans.

The second and most important overall feature of the Cuban economic enclave in Miami is its institutional range. In effect, the variety of sales and services controlled by Cubans, as well as their penetration into the professions, is so extensive that some claim it is possible for Miami Cubans to live completely within the ethnic community. That is not literally true. Almost all Cubans interact extensively with mainstream American institutions, specifically the state, to which they pay taxes and which educates most of their children. But the claim does reflect something about the extensiveness of the Cuban economic enclave.

The relatively all-encompassing character of the enclave somewhat insulates the newly-arrived Latino immigrants from the usual vicissitudes of the secondary labor market. In contrast to Mexican immigrants in the United States, for example, who join the labor market in peripheral sectors of the economy dominated by Anglos and with little informal support, many recent Cuban immigrants enter the labor market largely through businesses owned or operated by earlier Cuban arrivals. While wages may not be higher in the enclave than in the mainstream economy, ethnic bonds provide informal networks of support that facilitate learning new skills, gaining access to resources, and the overall process of economic adjustment. These positive implications have helped Cubans attain a socioeconomic position which is relatively high in comparison with most other immigrant groups.

While Cuban entrepreneurship is impressive, it should be noted that most businesses are small and family-owned. Only one out of seven Hispanic businesses in Miami in 1990 had paid employees and together they generated only 30,000 paid jobs (Metro-Dade County 1993). Cubans remain under-represented in the fastest growing industries, especially financial services. Although their representation has increased, they continue to be outnumbered by Anglos in professional and executive occupations. Indeed, Cubans in Miami are over-represented in manual occupations, working primarily as laborers, craftsmen, and service workers.

Recently-arrived Cuban immigrants are likely to find their first job in Miami working for other Cubans (Portes, Manning, and Clark, 1986). Working for co-ethnics offers the advantages of requiring no language training and the opportunity to work with compatriots. For the employers, the new immigrants offer a cheap source of labor. Javier's experience as a "Marielito," a Cuban arriving in 1980 during the Mariel boatlift, is typical of many trying to get a footing in Cuban Miami. Now he works at a mattress factory owned by a Cuban, but when we interviewed him a few years back, he recalled his initial experience in Miami.

> After I got here, many people helped us. My mother-in-law and my cousin told me how I had to act to make my way here. They bought us food and clothes. We lived with them for four months. It was practically like our home. They'd cook for us and for their family. They also gave us money for our necessities and to buy some things. They had a cafeteria and they gave us work there. I kept working there until I could find something better. At the same time, they introduced us to other people who might need employees in their businesses. I worked real hard and it wasn't always easy but I can't complain. They helped us a good deal.

Working for other Cubans is not always a piece of cake. Frequently working conditions are informal, that is, in violation of labor laws and much like those endured by the most exploited undocumented aliens in other parts of the United States (Stepick 1989 and 1990; Fernandez-Kelly and Garcia 1989). In the restaurant industry, many Cubans have employed their recently-arrived compatriots at less than the minimum wage.

But the enclave seems to provide a leg up for many new arrivals. For example, immigrants who arrived in the mid 1970s and the Mariel Cubans who arrived in 1980 both had poverty level incomes for a few years after they arrived (Portes and Bach 1985; Portes and Stepick 1985). But within three years, their incomes had improved notably, with 1970s immigrant Cubans advancing more quickly than a comparable group of Mexican immigrants and 1980 Mariel Cubans outstripping comparable Haitian immigrants in Miami.

In contrast to recently-arrived Cuban male workers, Cuban females generally continue to have low incomes long after they arrive. Cuban female annual income in the United States in 1979 was scarcely higher than for the total U.S. Hispanic female population (Bernal 1982; Ferree 1979; Kurtines and Miranda 1980; Pérez 1986b, 10; Prieto 1987; Szapocznik and Fernandez 1988; Szapocznik, Scopetta, Tillman 1978). While both male and female Cuban immigrants may begin working in informal jobs in the enclave, men appear to be more capable of advancing out of those jobs, while women remain in them. During the 1980s, as the number of female-headed households increased among Cubans, poverty rates also rose. In our discussion below of Cuban social capital, we will indicate how low incomes among females, however, creates less poverty in the Miami Cuban community that it does in other U.S. Hispanic communities.

Those Cubans most likely to be poor are the elderly. Elderly Cubans in Miami receive more public assistance than other U.S. Hispanics. There is also simply a higher proportion of elderly among U.S. Cubans than among other U.S. Hispanics. In 1990, more than one-third of the Cuban population in the U.S. was fifty or older and the average age of the Cuban-origin population was more than fifteen years higher than that of the total U.S. Hispanic population (40.5 versus 25.5). In Miami, traditionally a retirement center for whites from the U.S. northeast, more than a third of the area's elderly population is Cuban (Dluhy and Krebs 1987).

Thus, success has not been shared by all Cubans. The typical Cuban in Miami is more likely to be working class and, nationally, poverty among Cubans is nearly twice as high as non-Hispanic white poverty. Miami Cuban females earn low incomes and the Cuban elderly in Miami have higher poverty rates than Miami's African Americans. Yet, the vast majority of Cubans in Miami have not become welfare dependent and have achieved more on average than other U.S. Hispanics. This is largely due to the types of capital that the Cubans have been able to exploit.

TYPES OF CAPITAL

The favorable macro social, political, and economic conditions that welcomed the Cubans to the United States certainly helped shape the fate of Cuban immigrants, but they also had skills and talents that allowed them to take advantage of the favorable conditions. Cubans have had three forms of capital: economic, political, and social. By capital, we mean available resources that can be invested or utilized to produce even more assets. The three types of capital interacted to construct an ethnic solidarity that in turn reinforced and strengthened Cuban immigrants' capital.

Economic Capital

Cubans who arrived in the United States in the 1960s, when the foundations for community were laid, were disproportionately drawn from the upper sectors of Cuban society. Many were professionals or entrepreneurs and had university degrees. A significant proportion had previous business experience, and more than a few had contacts with U.S. companies that had done business in Cuba before the revolution. Most shared a belief in the superiority of capitalism, a confidence in their own abilities, and a positive regard for the United States. As elites, they often had close personal and family ties with others who had arrived earlier, and some had moved their capital to the United States prior to arrival, depositing it in banks or investing in real estate. Yet others were able to land jobs with American companies (Perez-Stable and Uriarte 1990, 5). This fortunate minority sometimes provided a leg up for later arrivals, furnishing "character loans" based less on income statements than on trust, honor, and personal knowledge that the individuals in question were skilled and motivated and had a history of business success in pre-revolutionary Cuba (Portes and Stepick 1993, 132–134).

Not all Anglos in Miami looked favorably upon the Spanish-speaking newcomers from the south, no matter what their politics, and Cubans did encounter a measure of prejudice and discrimination, as Pepe's story above indicates. Still, given the nature of racism in the United States and in Miami, white Anglo employers in Miami often preferred to hire a white former Cuban teacher, pharmacist, or office worker with a heavy Spanish accent than an African American. As one Miami African American put it:

> When they [Cubans] first came, white folks welcomed them; they welcomed them because, according to [the whites] we, the Blacks, had forgotten our place. We had gotten very sassy and non-dependable and non-reliable; they found themselves having to deal with a new minority called Cubans and that was good for them because, once again, they had access to a cheaper pool of labor for the hotels, motels and restaurants.

Many Cubans were forced to work at low wage jobs when they first arrived, much like most Mexican immigrants and Puerto Ricans. But the two other forms of Cuban capital, political and social, meant that most Cubans did not stay long in these entry level positions.

Political Capital

American attitudes toward immigrants were fairly positive in the early 1960s, in the wake of postwar prosperity and a period of very low immigration, and there was a special sympathy for refugees fleeing from communism. Refugee communities frequently garner political capital since the very status of refugee reflects a political decision by the receiving state. In the United States, groups designated as refugees are offered special governmental assistance when they arrive that is not available to other immigrant flows (Loescher and Scanlan 1986; Zucker and Zucker 1987). Such was the case with the Cubans.

The U.S. government created for the arriving Cubans an unprecedented direct and indirect assistance program, the Cuban Refugee Program, that spent nearly $1 billion between 1965 and 1976 (Pedraza-Bailey 1985, 41). The federal government provided transportation costs from Cuba, financial assistance to needy refugees and to state and local public agencies that provided services for refugees, and employment and professional training courses for refugees. During the 1960s, the IRS allowed Cubans to declare capital losses for properties in Cuba (Perez-Stable and Uriarte 1990, 6). Even in programs not especially designed for them, Cubans seemed to benefit. From 1968 to 1980, Hispanics (almost all Cubans) received 46.9 percent of all Small Business Administration loans in Dade County (Porter and Dunn 1984, 196).

A second government program that unintentionally provided resources that assisted Cuban success was the U.S. covert war against the Castro government. The vast operation run out of Miami by the Central Intelligence Agency in the early 1960s meant an infusion of cash into the local Cuban community. The University of Miami had the largest CIA station in the world outside of the organization's headquarters in Virginia. With perhaps as many as 12,000 Cubans in Miami on the CIA payroll at one point in the early 1960s, it was one of the largest employers in the state of Florida. It supported what was described as the third-largest navy in the world and over fifty front businesses: CIA boat shops, CIA gun shops, CIA travel agencies, CIA detective agencies, and CIA real-estate agencies (Didion 1987, 90–91; Rieff 1987, 193–207; Rich 1974, 7–9). In addition, hundreds of Cubans were trained in undercover operations, and when the U.S. government cut off funding in the late 1960s, some of them became involved in the lucrative drug trade. While it is a gross distortion to see the Cuban success story as a mere result of U.S. government support based on Cold War considerations plus CIA and drug money, there is little doubt that these factors contributed seed capital for at least some legitimate enterprises. In our interview with Javier, mentioned above, the owner of the mattress factory that currently employs him received his start in the United States by working for the CIA after arriving in the 1960s.

These benefits, moreover, were not limited to those the federal government provided. The State of Florida passed laws that made it easier for Cuban professionals, especially medical doctors, to re-certify themselves to practice in the United States. At the county level, in the late 1970s and early 1980s, 53 percent of minority con-tracts for Dade County's rapid transit system went to Hispanic, mostly Cuban, firms. Dade County Schools led the nation in bilin-gual education by introducing it for the first wave of Cuban refugees in 1960. The Dade County Commission also designated the county officially bilingual in the mid 1970s. Cubans in Miami had available especially for them language classes, vocational training, business education, and varied adult education programs (Mohl 1990, 49).

In sum, the total benefits available to the Cuban community ap-pear to surpass those available to other U.S. minority groups. About 75 percent of Cuban arrivals before 1974 directly received some kind of state-provided benefits (Pedraza-Bailey 1985, 40 based on Clark 1975, 116). Moreover, the presence of entrepreneurs and professionals in the Cuban refugee flow provided a trained and experienced core who knew how to access and use these privileges. Cuban family structure further encouraged the maximum exploitation of the new resources.

Social Capital

Cuban Miami is a prime example of an immigrant community high in social capital. Portes (1995, 257) defines social capital as "the abil-ity to command scarce resources by virtue of membership in net-works or broader social structures." At the core of the formation of immigrant social capital is a solidarity that is "grounded in a com-mon cultural memory and the replication of home country institu-tions" (Portes 1995, 258). In the case of Cuban Miami, that solidarity is bonded even more strongly than in many other immigrant com-munities by the experience of exile, which sharpens Cubans' sense of a common history and, even further, a common purpose as a group. Portes and Stepick (1993, 137–138) viewed this as a major feature of the Cuban enclave in Miami and labeled it "the moral community." Furthermore, exiles, holding out the hope of recovering the home-land, strive to transplant and replicate the institutions of the country of origin, contributing to that sense of group solidarity.

This degree of solidarity is further reinforced by the economic benefits of the enclave, resulting in a multiplication of social net-works within the community. The dense social networks of Cuban Miami provide a tremendous asset which members of the commu-nity can use to advance their agenda of upward mobility for them-selves and, especially, for their children (Portes 1995, 258). They also reinforce the immigrants' values, norms, ideology, and shield them from discrimination from the dominant society. In short, what social capital does is give a positive value to being a Cuban in Miami.

The social capital of the Cuban community is evident throughout its institutions. But it is most evident in the family, which is at the core of the dense social networks within the enclave and is a crucial resource in implementing upward mobility, reinforcing the culture of the home country, and promoting community solidarity (see Chapter 5).

CONCLUSION

Cubans are regarded as exceptional Hispanics in the United States—their average income is relatively high, and poverty rates and dependency on welfare are relatively low. It is rare to see a first generation of newcomers obtain the economic and political success that the Cubans have achieved. At a minimum, Cubans demonstrate that general community poverty and marginalization are not inherent to Spanish-speaking communities or recent immigrant minority groups. Nor does massive state-funded assistance programs necessarily fuel economic dependency. In at least this one case, such programs have produced a successful ethnic enclave.

Yet, the Cuban success story is partly a result of being in the right place at the right time. As traumatic as leaving Cuba was for most of the early migrants, at least they arrived in a country which was ready to receive them and reap the benefits. It is very likely that the open-arm reception was fueled partly by the belief, and hope, that the exiles would soon return to their homeland, sentiments that were shared by most exiles as well. But Cubans made the most of the resources offered and, forty years later, we can see how the numerous assistance programs and the special historical conditions and characteristics of the immigrants contributed to this pattern. In many ways, Miami too was ready for a group like the Cubans—a group that could take the region's frontier character, established by northern snowbirds and seasonal capital, and shape it in its image, as the Cubans have. The arrivals from the island, and their Cuban American offspring, have made the United States their land, and Miami their capital.

5

Family Business

Kinship and Economic Adjustment

Nildita Vilariño admits that the restaurant business is not her passion. She says, however, that it is a "family commitment." Her four sisters, Vilma, Irina, Miriam, and Carmen, agree. The Vilariño family arrived in Florida through the Mariel boatlift in 1980, when most of the five sisters were young children. They now own nine restaurants scattered throughout southern Florida, serving moderately-priced Cuban and Mexican food.

They started their business in 1984 when their father, Antonio, and their mother, Nilda, invested all their savings in purchasing a rundown cafeteria. But there was no money left for remodeling or for employees.

> [The] daughters helped with the painting, the floor tiling and the carpentry. They were also the waitresses, kitchen helpers, and clean-up crew.... They did their homework when there were no customers around. On the weekends, everyone worked full shifts. "There were no Friday night parties or Saturday football games," said Vilma, now 30. As a high school student she dreamed of becoming a cheerleader. The family joke is that Vilma's job was to cheer on the customers so they would return.... The five sisters say they are grateful to their parents for teaching them the value of hard work, and as Vilma puts it, "it's nice to be the boss." Each daughter supervises at least two restaurants and Vilma runs the central office.... Today, the Vilariños enjoy the perks of their success, which include custom-built homes with swimming pools. They live within walking distance of each other and they get together at least once a day, usually at night at the parents' home. (Ramirez 2000)

Not all Cuban American families own successful businesses, but the story of the Vilariño family serves to underscore the role of the family in the process of economic adjustment in the United States, and especially its role in the development of the relatively high incidence of entrepreneurship among Cubans in the United States. One way to look at the Cuban American family is as a unit that is structured in a manner that facilities upward social mobility and economic success.

MIGRATION AND FAMILY STRUCTURE

We have already presented the extraordinary conditions that have shaped Cuban migration to the United States over the past two centuries, especially during the last four decades of the twentieth century. Those conditions have determined the characteristics and dynamics of the Cuban presence in the United States, a presence that stands as one exception to the general picture of U.S. immigration. In many ways, the Cuban American family reflects those extraordinary conditions.

Although it is difficult to generalize across all the postrevolutionary migration waves from Cuba, the first two waves (the Early Exiles, 1959–1962, and the Airlift, 1965–1973) established in the United States patterns of family organization that persist to this day. As the Vilariño family demonstrates, those patterns are also found among many of the later arrivals, for they are patterns shaped by certain constant features of Cuban immigration and of the adjustment of Cubans in this country.

The Socioeconomic Selectivity of the Migration

As has already been noted, the revolutionary process and the intense class struggle of the early 1960s resulted in the alienation of Cuba's elite and its overrepresentation in the ensuing exodus. Throughout the 1960s and into the early 1970s, emigration peeled away the layers of the Cuban class system, stating at the top and eventually reaching deep into the middle sectors. This meant that Cuban immigrants have been drawn disproportionately from the most "modernized" sectors of Cuban society, a society that underwent a rapid modernization process during the first half of the twentieth century largely because of the pervasive influence of the United States. Urbanization occurred at a rapid pace, fertility and mortality dropped sharply, per capita income was relatively high, and consumer goods from the United States were widely available (Díaz-Briquets 1983; Díaz-Briquets and Pérez 1981; International Bank for Reconstruction and Development 1951, 35–42; Marrero 1987). The Catholic Church, a historically weak institution in Cuba, did not serve as an effective bulwark against a sweeping tide of secularism (Pérez 1994a, 147–157). By the close of the nineteenth century, neolocality became the norm, and the transition was underway from the traditional patriarchal marriage to one based more on egalitarianism and companionship (Aguirre 1981, 400). Those indicators of modernization were not, of course, equally evident throughout the social class system, but it was precisely the most modernized sectors of Cuban society that participated massively in the postrevolutionary exodus.

The modernization of twentieth-century Cuba is especially apparent in the family-related legislation enacted from the 1930s to the 1950s, legislation that significantly altered and liberalized the very traditional Spanish Civil Code. A 1930 law, for example, made "mutual consent" a valid ground for divorce and permitted the granting of divorces simply upon the request of both parties (República de Cuba 1939, 2189–2193).

The 1940 Constitution included a clause that affirmed a married woman's full civil status, recognizing her right to freely exercise "commerce, industry, profession, or occupation without marital license or authorization," as well as to freely dispose of the fruits of her labor. Subsequent legislation, enacted in the 1950s, served to increase the legal status of women in a number of areas (República de Cuba 1950, 27553–27554).

While the social reality fell far short of the attempts to legislate equality between men and women, these progressive family statutes reflect a society that by mid-twentieth century was at the vanguard of most of Latin America in the level of modernization of its values and norms. The more privileged and modernized segments of that society formed the catalyst and the core of the postrevolutionary exodus.

The Demographic Selectivity of the Migration

If there is such a thing as a "typical" U.S. immigrant, it is likely to be a young unmarried male migrating without a family. While there are increasing exceptions to that profile, that combination of age, sex, and marital status continues to be the norm, especially among labor migrants. The post-1959 exodus from Cuba, however, has a profile that is diametrically opposed to that "typical" profile.

The revolutionary transformation Cuba experienced in the early 1960s led to an exodus in which young families tended to predominate, fearful of the implications of the changes for their children. In fact, thousands of unaccompanied children were sent ahead to the United States to await reunification with their parents. The political context of the Cuban exodus meant that there were a very high number of entire family units within the migration flow from Cuba, especially in the early years.

The Airlift (1965–1973), as also noted previously, brought a disproportionately large number of the elderly and women, as the Cuban government prohibited the emigration of males of military age and gave priority for exit visas to the elderly, who by that time had decided to join their children and grandchildren who had emigrated some years before. The result is that the Cuban population of the United States is older and with proportionately more females than most immigrant groups.

"QUÉ PASA USA?"

From 1977 to 1979 a group of writers, producers, and actors, most of them based in Miami, crafted a series of programs of a low-budget bilingual television sitcom they called *"Qué Pasa USA?"* Sponsored and initially transmitted by the Public Television station in Miami, the series was based on the comical (and sometimes plaintive) misadventures of a family of Cuban immigrants adjusting to life in 1970s Miami. The series met with unexpected success because its creators crafted the fictional Peña family in a manner so faithful to the social reality around them that Cuban Americans could see themselves mirrored in the situations, triumphs, and trials of the Peñas. To this day it is continually being rebroadcast by public and cable television stations in Miami and in many cities throughout the country.

The head of the family was (unquestionably) José (Pepe) Peña, a blue collar worker in his early forties who is always struggling to maintain in his family the traditional values and norms of the Cuba in which he grew up, especially male authority, the double standard of morality, and the proper roles of husbands, wives, daughters, and sons. In this country, Pepe faces an uphill battle as his traditional beliefs are constantly under siege. His wife Juana is generally traditional and subservient, but she works outside the home and frequently finds occasion to successfully challenge or subvert her husband's authority, especially in covert ways.

Pepe and Juana arrived in the United States in the 1960s with their two young children, José Jr. ("Joe") and Carmencita, who by the time we catch up with them in the 1970s are teenagers in high school. Bilingual and bicultural, Joe and Carmencita constantly face the conflicting normative expectations of the outside "American" world and their parents' traditional Cuban world and provide much of the cultural counterpoint on which the series thrives. They are the principal sources of the challenges to Pepe's traditionalism.

The influence of the home country is reinforced by Juana's parents, Adela and Antonio, who also live in the family's modest Miami home. The elderly couple, who no doubt arrived through the Airlift a few years after Pepe and Juana, represent bulwarks of Cuban ways, but unlike their daughter and son-in-law, their ages make them immune to any expectation that they need to adjust to the ways of a new country. They are usually baffled and bewildered when they confront the unfamiliar, to which they are ultimately impervious. They are nostalgic for the lost homeland, a place far superior, of course, to the new world they now face. "*Qué Pasa USA?*" so brilliantly portrayed and encapsulated the experience of Cuban American families during the first couple of decades after their arrival in the United States, that it can serve as a prototype for presenting the principal features of the family organization of Cubans in this country, features that largely persist to this day.

The Three-Generation Household and the Contribution of the Elderly

The Peña household was certainly not the only Cuban American family with three generations. The many elderly persons who arrived during the Airlift were in a vulnerable situation, culturally and economically, in adjusting to life in this country. It would have been difficult to face that adjustment as heads of households. Furthermore, their children followed the traditional Cuban cultural norm that it is disgraceful to have one's parents living alone or in nursing homes. For Pepe and Juana, it would have been unthinkable to let her parents live anywhere but in their home.

The 1980 U.S. Census, taken around the time the Peñas were on television, contains an extraordinary finding. One-fourth of all Cuban-born persons sixty-five years of age and over lived in households in which they are parents or parents-in-law of the head of the household. By comparison, less than 8 percent of all elderly persons in the United States lived in such household arrangements. Furthermore, although in 1980 6 percent of all elderly in this country lived in "group quarters" (such as nursing homes), less than one percent of Cuban-born elderly lived in group quarters.

In "*Qué Pasa USA?*" Antonio and Adela were never portrayed as a burden to the family. In fact, that elderly generation contributed in many ways to the economic well-being of the household. Although they had virtually no Social Security income because of their limited work experience in the United States, they were eligible for various federal and state assistance programs, including benefits from the Cuban Refugee Program (Queralt 1983, 55–56). Such assistance would have barely covered Antonio and Adela's expenses had they lived by themselves, but as members of the three-generation Peña household, their economic contribution from public sources helped to raise the family's total income. According to the 1980 U.S. Census, the proportion of Cuban households receiving public assistance was relatively high, and nearly three-fourths of households receiving such assistance were above the poverty level. This datum is consistent with the relative importance of the three-generation family among Cubans, in that the income of the elderly was more likely to contribute to a household that included employed persons.

But perhaps the greatest economic contribution of the elderly was as caretakers of their grandchildren, facilitating the employment of their daughters or daughters-in-law. Although by the late 1970s Joe and Carmencita are already teenagers, no doubt Adela and Antonio served as their caretakers in the children's younger years, allowing Juana to work outside the home, further raising the family's income.

Antonio and Adela also had an impact on the Peña family in ways that went beyond the economic. As the immutable bastions of the culture of the home country, they were critical in exposing Joe and Carmencita to that culture, acting as buffers to the younger generation's rapid assimilation. In one survey, the Children of Immigrants Longitudinal Study (CILS), Cuban-origin children living in Miami with at least one grandparent in the household expressed higher levels of competency in Spanish than those children who do not live with a grandparent (Pérez 1996, 114–115).

By now, the number of three-generation families has declined among U.S. Cubans. This decline was to be expected: Adela and Antonio have probably already died, and now the elderly couple are Pepe and Juana; however, the economic and cultural context is very different from twenty years ago. Unlike the situation of Juana's parents, Pepe and Juana will be entering retirement age after decades of active employment in this country, which means they will probably have retirement benefits that will keep them financially (and residentially) independent of their children. It is likely that they have become sufficiently "acculturated" to U.S. norms to prefer living on their own. In any case, Joe and Carmencita, who grew up in this country and are now middle-aged, are probably not as receptive as Pepe and Juana were twenty years ago to having parents living with them.

Aging and Retirement

The aging of the contemporaries of Pepe and Juana is one of the most important features of the Cuban American population. They came in the 1960s as young adults, and especially as parents of young children, and they are the largest cohort among Cuban Americans. Now between the ages of fifty-five and seventy-four, they account for more than one-fourth of all Cuban-origin persons and nearly one-half of all the Cuban-born in the United States. Presently, about 30 percent of the Cuban-born are over sixty-five. The aging of this large cohort is most evident in southern Florida, where providing services for the elderly is a booming business. In comparison with Cubans living elsewhere in the United States, the population of Cubans in southern Florida is even older. In fact, the rapid aging of the population has even contributed to the process of concentration in southern Florida. Many in that large age cohort that includes Pepe and Juana were resettled away from Miami in the 1960s by the U.S. government's Cuban Refugee Program. As they have reached retirement age, a large proportion of them have chosen to return to Miami to live out their lives in a warmer climate and in a community with a large population of co-ethnics.

Female Employment

Juana worked outside the home, in a factory, as did many Cuban women of her generation. At the time *"Qué Pasa USA?"* was on the air, and the women of Juana's cohort were in productive ages, Cuban American women tended to work outside the home, despite the fact that many of these women had no history of employment in Cuba.

Relatively high female labor force participation rates continue to characterize the U.S. Cuban population. By the end of the twentieth

Playing cards (and kibitzing) in a park in Little Havana. About 30 percent of the Cuban-born in the United States are over 65 years of age and the population is aging rapidly.

(Peggy Levison Nolan)

century, a majority of all Cuban-origin women were economically active, despite the aging of the population, which undoubtedly pushed women of Juana's cohort into retirement and out of the labor force.

It would be a mistake to attribute the high rates of female labor force participation in the United States to egalitarian gender roles. Although there probably has been a trend toward egalitarianism, especially among new generations of Cuban Americans, research has shown that among Cubans in the United States, high rates of female employment co-exist with fairly traditional orientations regarding the role of women in society and the appropriateness of their employment outside the home. For women, employment has been largely viewed as purely instrumental in assisting and furthering the family's economic status (Ferree 1979, 44–45 and Prieto 1987, 85). Juana worked in the *factoría* in order to contribute to the Peña household income so that the family could get ahead and do well in the new country. Women of Juana's generation, who arrived as adults from Cuba and probably had never worked outside the home in their country, usually settled into blue-collar jobs without aspirations for career advancement (Portes and Stepick 1993, 128). The 1980 U.S. Census showed that Juana's *factoría* job was all-too typical: the modal employment category for U.S. Cuban women that year was nondurable manufacturing.

The Cuban enclave in Miami undoubtedly facilitated the entry of women into the labor force, providing "acceptable" employment venues. Family businesses have been one such venue, employing women within the context of a family enterprise, as was the case with the Vilariño family. Juana's factory work was also facilitated by the enclave: the bulk of the *factorías* usually had Cuban managers, its workforces were homogenous in terms of both ethnicity and gender, and recruitment was done through informal networks, guaranteeing that the women working there were surrounded by relatives or friends. Those kinship and peer connections made factory work more acceptable and accessible to women. Another factor that contributed to high rates of female employment was South Florida's economy, with its predominance of precisely those sectors that employ women: retail sales, services, and nondurable manufacturing (Pérez 1986b, 17).

Although Juana and her generation had undoubtedly already retired by the end of the twentieth century, blue-collar employment continues to be important among women who arrive as adults from Cuba, especially the post-Mariel arrivals. Younger generations of Cuban women, however, those born in the United States or those arriving very young from the island, are likely to have obtained the training and education to enter the professional ranks. Had *"Qué Pasa USA?"* continued, we would have undoubtedly seen Carmencita go to college and become a professional. Cubans in the United

Cuban women in a Miami *factoría*. Non-durable manufacturing has traditionally been a major employer of Cuban-born women in South Florida.

(Peggy Levison Nolan)

States have demonstrated that they share high expectations of social mobility in this country, and, especially, high aspirations for intergenerational mobility. Those aspirations are sufficiently high to trump any traditional objections to the career aspirations of daughters. Pepe and Juana would have been greatly disappointed if Carmencita had followed Juana's footsteps to the *factoría*.

Low Birth Rate

In terms of the number of children, the fictional two-child Peña family is, ironically, more representative of the reality of Cuban Americans than the real-life Vilariño family (with its five daughters). At the time *"Qué Pasa USA?"* was in production, the U.S. Census of 1980 revealed that the number of children ever born to women of Cuban origin was extraordinarily low, lower even than the number of children born to white women living in U.S. metropolitan areas (Pérez 1994b, 101). That trend was established largely by Juana's generation of immigrant Cuban women, who were disproportionately drawn from the most modernized sectors of Cuban society and who in this country had both the aspirations and expectations of upward mobility, as their labor force participation rates clearly demonstrate.

The 1990 Census showed that a low birth rate was an enduring trend, extending to a younger generation of Cuban American women. It was very unlikely that Carmencita would have had more than two children. In fact, by the year 2000, the five Vilariño sisters, who then ranged in age from twenty-four to thirty-eight, had given birth to only four children (and even then, two of the four were twins!).

This low level of reproduction is a factor that has both responded to and, in turn, contributed to, the relatively successful economic adjustment of many Cubans in the United States. Having children can have a negative impact on upward mobility, and Cuban American couples have apparently chosen to reduce their birth rate. Having fewer children, in turn, facilitates female employment, which remains high. A low birth rate has kept the Cuban American family relatively small. Once the generation of Adela and Antonio, who lived with their children, starting dying off, the average size of the Cuban household plummeted.

Marital Instability

Pepe and Juana never divorced, but one of the pervasive subthemes of *"Qué Pasa USA?"* dealt with the pressures their marriage faced as they adjusted to a new society. Although such pressures may be found among many immigrants, the first waves of Cuban exiles perceived that they were compelled to leave the island. As "reluctant" immigrants, they faced special problems in their psychosocial adjustment to the new country. Furthermore, given the initial socioeconomic selectivity of the exodus, and despite the subsequent economic success of many in this country, there is no doubt that most experienced drastic downward mobility when they first arrived. Such downward mobility may have redefined and strained marital relations. The secularism and modernism of Cuban migrants, the value placed on upward mobility, the postponement of childbearing and low fertility, and the tendency to settle in a rapidly-changing metropolitan area, have combined to establish and maintain rates of marital disruption higher than would be expected for a Latin American immigrant population. To all this one must add the conflicts inherent in the high rates of female employment within a gender-role context that is still fairly traditional. Cuban women have the double burden of employment and domestic responsibility, creating a structural condition conducive to marital conflict.

Among Cuban Americans, the relatively high incidence of marital dissolution has not translated into family characteristics usually associated with a high divorce rate. Cuban Americans do not tend to have many female-headed households. Most children under eighteen live with both parents. Two fairly traditional patterns appear to be operating here. One is that single Cuban women tend not to live separately from their parents, so that when women divorce they are likely to return to their parents' household. The other is that couples with children are not as likely to divorce as couples without children. Consequently, the return of many divorced women to the parental home is facilitated by the high incidence of childlessness among divorced couples. Furthermore, a fairly large number of childless couples is one way the divorce rate can remain high despite the inhibiting effect that the presence of children has on marital breakups.

Census data show that a high divorce rate is a persistent problem, with newer generations of Cuban Americans entering the marital ages experiencing a high incidence of marital dissolution. Had the show continued, no doubt the writers of *"Qué Pasa USA?"* would have introduced divorce as part of the life of at least one of the Peña children. By 2000, only two of the five Vilariño sisters were married. Two were divorced and another had not married.

THE FAMILY AND ECONOMIC ADJUSTMENT

Although the Cuban "success story" in the United States has frequently been exaggerated, oversimplifying the complexity and diversity of the Cuban American reality, the data do indicate that along every measure of family income and economic well-being there is some basis for the image of successful adjustment.

Clearly, the initial socioeconomic selectivity of the migration and the subsequent establishment of a thriving enclave in Miami are major factors responsible for that success. But it is also important to recognize that those factors have largely operated through the family, which has organizational features that facilitate upward mobility: high female employment rates, low birth rates, and the contribution of the elderly in three-generation households. The achievement orientation of Cuban Americans is also evident in one additional feature of the Cuban household: despite having a large number of workers per family, Cubans under thirty-five years of age exhibit rates of school enrollment that are superior to the enrollment figures for the total United States and Spanish populations.

Cubans can be said, then, to have a "family work ethic." As such, the Cuban "success story," at least at the individual level, has been overstated. The key to the economic achievements of Cuban immigrants lies in the apparently high degree of economic cooperation within the family. It is a family whose principal characteristics are tailored to facilitate upward mobility: a relatively large number of workers, high rates of female employment, the presence, at least initially, of an elderly generation that contributed directly and indirectly to the household's financial resources, and high levels of school enrollment.

Cubans, of course, are certainly not unique among immigrant groups in having high expectations and aspirations for upward mobility in their adopted country. In the case of Cubans, however, the initial socioeconomic selectivity of the migration and the accompanying high levels of modernity and secularism have readily permitted the enactment of family strategies consistent with those expectations and aspirations. Few other immigrant groups, at least upon first arriving, have had such favorable demographic and socioeconomic forces facilitating their adjustment to this country. Those same correlates of modernity and secularism that have served Cubans well in the process of economic adjustment have also, however, resulted in a higher incidence of marital instability.

For Cubans in Miami, the enclave, as noted, has facilitated many features of the organization of the Cuban family in Miami, especially the employment of women. But the family, in turn, has had a formative impact on the very creation of the enclave. At the core of the enclave is the development of a diversified range of entrepreneurial activities so that its members can live out the entirety of their lives within the enclave (Portes and Bach 1985, 203–204). Indeed, Miami has by far the largest number of Hispanic-owned businesses of any city in the United States.

As Portes and Stepick have noted (1993, 136–137), the precarious financial beginnings of most Cuban businesses in Miami required low-cost family labor willing to work long hours. The Vilariño family built its entire chain of restaurants on the labor of the father, mother, and five daughters. While not all Cuban families own successful businesses, the existence of so many Cuban-owned firms in Miami is in no small measure due to families who overcame shortage of capital through their own pooled labor.

The Cuban American family, therefore, is a cornerstone of two of the most prominent features of the Cuban presence in the United States: fairly successful economic adjustment and the creation of a true ethnic enclave.

CONCLUSION

When Antonio Vilariño was asked to give the reason for the success of his restaurant business, his answer was not surprising: family unity (Ramirez 2000, 5G). Without a strong family entrepreneurial ethic and the sacrifice of his wife and five daughters, the business could never have flourished. The Cuban American family has played a critical role in the generally successful economic adjustment of Cubans in the United States. A strong ethnic enclave and the socioeconomic and demographic selectivity of their migration to the

United States have created contexts favorable to the successful implementation of that family entrepreneurial ethic.

The popularity of *"Qué Pasa USA?"* was largely due to the identification of the viewers with the Peña family. Every episode was the story of yet another challenge that the family faced in the process of adjusting to a new country and culture. The Peñas faced their travails with humor and, in the end, triumphed over them, largely through family cohesion. Success through reliance on the family was a theme that struck close to the experience of most Cuban American viewers.

6

Hanging Together, Hanging Alone

Relations between Cubans and Others in Miami

In the winter of 1989, in the wake of yet another crisis in interethnic relations in Miami, the Greater Miami Chamber of Commerce held its annual Goals Conference in a resort in the Florida Keys. Part of the conference's program included a meeting of the Chamber's Hispanic Affairs Committee, composed almost entirely of prominent Cuban American businessmen. The relaxed beach setting did nothing to alleviate the tension in the room as committee members engaged in an emotional and soul-searching discussion about their place within the Chamber.

"There is too little Hispanic influence and too few Hispanic committee chairs even though there are now a large number of Hispanics in the Chamber," said one committee member. "You cannot solve these problems by talking solely among Hispanics in this committee which is 99 percent Hispanic. All four groups, Blacks, Anglos, Hispanics, and Jews must be brought together in a seminar to talk about the issues. I do not believe in the melting pot. We can't seem to get together in this community."

Another Committee member demurred: "Do we need a separate committee? Do we have separate goals? We should not have this apartheid. This is not South Africa."

One of Miami's most successful and respected Cuban bankers pointedly disagreed: "I'm not so sure the situation is different than South Africa."

It is difficult to reconcile this type of attitude with the alleged success that Cuban Americans have enjoyed in the United States. Aren't these the leaders of a community that has achieved unparalleled success in one generation? Hasn't the door of opportunity swung off its hinges for these New Americans? What is this talk about "apartheid" between Cubans and Anglos in Miami?

CUBANS AND THE WHITE BUSINESS ELITE: IT'S NOT YOUR FATHER'S CHAMBER OF COMMERCE

As it turns out, these Cuban leaders are complaining about having to sleep in the bed they've made. Cuban American business leaders prospered in Miami by not joining mainstream "American" business organizations. Rather than becoming part of the Greater Miami Chamber of Commerce, they participated in the Cámara de Comercio Latina (CAMACOL). Rather than petitioning for entry into the South Florida Builders' Association, they formed the Latin Builders' Association. Rather than contributing to the American Cancer Society, they supported La Liga Contra el Cancer.

In this process, two parallel "White" elites, separate but equal, emerged. The Cubans maintained a low profile, developed their associations and patiently waited for the downfall of Castro. The so-called "Anglo" elite watched from its perch, engaging the Cubans when necessary but primarily adjusting business plans to accommodate for the changing demographics.

But from the 1980s onward, White "American" leaders could no longer ignore Miami's Cubans, and Cubans were outgrowing the reach of their own organizations. Although not necessarily the equal of the White "American" elite in power and command of economic resources, the Miami Cuban elite had become a force. A 1988 study of top leadership conducted by *The Miami Herald* revealed the transformation. Of eighteen individuals identified as top leaders, ten were White "Americans" (56 percent). The other eight (44 percent) were all Miami Cubans. That was more than the Cuban share of the population of the metropolitan area. It was also more than the then White "American" share of the population.

While the economic and political power of Miami's Cubans grew visibly from 1980 on, certain events strikingly revealed how that power thwarted the interests of old line White "American" private sector leaders. In 1986 Miami's White "American" leadership proposed to add one cent to the local sales tax in order to finance the construction of a performing arts center. Cuban small businesses revolted. They saw no need for an extra penny from their customers to service White "American" elite needs. Cuban radio stations rallied against the initiative and for the first time in the White "American" elite's memory, one of their initiatives failed. A newspaper executive recounted that "The traditional leadership in Dade County had an ultimate comeuppance as far as Latinos are concerned. The day that penny sales tax was clobbered due to the leadership of the Latino Community—that was a watershed experience for the leadership of our community."

The defeat resolved the White "American" elite to abandon the policy of waiting for the Cubans to come to their side. The White "American" leadership could no longer afford the luxury of shutting out the Cubans. Besides needing support for political initiatives, Cuban customers were important for many businesses, as were Cuban executives, managers, and employees. Organizations such as United Way relied on contributions from Cuban workers and cooperation from Cuban managers and owners to meet their fund-raising goals. If White "Americans" continued to ignore Cubans, they could no longer advance their own agenda.

In response, an unspoken deal was cut. White "Americans" began to incorporate Cubans in elite circles, especially those Cubans who worked as executives in large "American" banks, corporations, and law firms. They elected Cubans to the chairmanships of key civic organizations such as the United Way of Dade County, the Orange Bowl Committee, and the GMCC. Hispanic, mostly Cuban, membership in the Chamber increased from about 5 percent at the beginning of the 1980s to over a third by 1989, the year the Hispanic Affairs Committee stuggled over inclusion in the Chamber.

White "American" leaders were proud of their inclusiveness. They felt that the leading civic organizations in Miami had become open to Cubans with the right talents and attitudes. A White "American" executive argued: "One group ought to be singled out, and that is the United Way. I really feel it represents the ultimate, positive dynamics of what a community ought to be. You have on that board all the groups, all parts of the community."

Since White "Americans" were extending themselves to incorporate Cubans, the continuation of parallel Cuban business and service institutions frequently frustrated White "American" elites. They felt as if they had opened all doors, sent all the appropriate invitations. In return, they expected assimilation into their organizations and the demise of alternative ethnic business organizations. They desired a unified business community with the White "Americans" in the lead and Cubans becoming Americans, speaking English and adopting what they viewed as American civic values.

There is no impediment for any Hispanic to be involved in anything they desire in Miami. There are no barriers. With intelligence and money anything can be achieved. But thousands don't want to get involved further than their activities in the Latin Chamber of Commerce. I just found out that Miami ranks 37th out of 50 in United Way contributions, and this is because a majority of citizens, Hispanics, don't care to give. All this is so sad, disappointing and a good barometer of how things are. United Way is a leveler, but even when headed by a Cuban one year, it didn't make any difference.

Although the White "American" leadership felt that "bringing the Cubans to the table" was progress, many Cubans increasingly felt a sense of ownership that contrasted sharply with the notion of them as outsiders being allowed into the game. With a growing power base of their own and substantial economic resources, many Cuban leaders could afford to decline what they perceived as condescending or patronizing invitations. A Miami media executive described the process: "The [White "American"] civic leadership invited *some* Latins to come to *their* place, sit at *their* table, and play by *their* rules."

For all the frustration with the Cubans, many in the White "American" elite view the "Cuban problem" as less severe and more transitional than the "Black problem." A top civic leader stated, "The biggest problem in Miami is the plight of the Blacks who live in a condition of stark poverty, suffer from racism, have a high rate of teenage pregnancies. I don't see any hope. Money alone will not solve the problem, but the lack of it makes things even worse."

AFRICAN AMERICANS AND CUBANS: DIVERGENT FATES

Gains by Black Miamians have paled by comparison with the economic success of Cubans. When Martin Luther King, Jr. visited Miami in 1966, he noted Miami's racial hostility and warned against pitting Cuban refugees against Blacks in competition for jobs (Porter and Dunn 1984). In the warning came the implicit understanding that given the intractability of racism, white, educated Cubans, providing cheap labor, might replace African Americans in the labor market. While this kind of displacement is difficult to document, as Portes and Stepick explain, "There was no one-to-one substitution of Blacks by Cubans...There was, however, a new urban economy in which the immigrants raced past other groups, leaving the native minority behind" (Portes and Stepick 1993, 43).

Four riots during the 1980s crystallized a widespread anger among Black Miamians over both their failure to keep pace economically with other groups and their lack of political voice (Herman 1995). The response of city elites was to create a series of economic and social programs designed to shore up Black neighborhoods (Reveron 1989). The task of rejuvenating the Black community was daunting, but there were some successes. Compared to a decade before, by 1987 the number of Black businesses had more than tripled.

Under a set-aside program Black contractors began receiving county work. In a gesture which might well symbolize what it takes to develop successful businesses in Miami's African American communities, Otis Pitts in 1999 received the MacArthur Foundation's "genius" award for building a shopping center on the border of Liberty City and Little Haiti which employed 130 people (Viglucci 1999). In general, development projects have met with limited success and gains in employment have been modest (Dunn and Stepick 1992). It could be generalized that most of the limited benefits from the special programs and incentives have gone to Black professionals and middle-class business people.

In the area of government minority contracts, Cubans clearly prevailed over Blacks. Between 1968 and 1980, the Small Business Administration (SBA) cumulatively dispersed 46.6 percent of its Dade County loans to Hispanics and only 6 percent to Blacks. The situation actually worsened after the riots when nearly 90 percent of the SBA loans were awarded to Hispanics or Whites. The Metro Miami Action Plan created to tap public and private resources for the development of Miami's Black community had only modest accomplishments and its elite Anglo participants soon lost interest (Dugger 1987).

Another area of conflict and division is business activity. According to the Minority Business Report of 1992, there were 926 Black-owned businesses with paid employees in Dade County. Their sales and receipts totaled $626.5 million, 0.5 percent of the total sales and receipts in Dade County—a considerably lower share than is typical of Black-owned business statewide or nationwide. Compare that to the 7,949 Cuban firms, which had sales and receipts of more than 7 billion. Even these figures underestimate the stagnation within the Black business community.

In 1982 African Americans owned one percent of all Miami-Dade County businesses. Now the number stands at 1.5 percent. Hispanics, on the other hand, already owned 11 percent of all businesses in 1987 and now own almost 17 percent. This antagonism echoes throughout the community. Until recently, Black leaders at county and state levels have persistently argued that Hispanics should not be included in minority set-asides.

But Miami's Cubans are quick to point out that the plight of the area's Black population predates the Cubans' arrival. They are right. In a chapter aptly entitled "Lost in the Fray," Portes and Stepick (1993, 178) document how "The story of Blacks in Miami has always been one of powerlessness, suffering, and frustrated attempts at resistance." During the first half of the twentieth century, strict southern segregationism was enforced and its legacy has been hard to erase. Before the civil rights legislation of the 1960s, the only Blacks allowed to stay overnight on Miami Beach were live-in servants. Before the arrival of the Cubans, most workers in the hotels and restaurants on the Beach were Black. They were required to carry identification cards and return to their homes across the bay each night. Entertainment stars appearing in Miami Beach hotels, such as Nat King Cole and Sammy Davis, Jr., had to stay in hotels in the predominantly Black neighborhood of Overtown. Apartheid endured into the early 1960s, when Miami scored about 99 on the residential segregation index (where 100 signifies total segregation), making it the most segregated metropolitan area in the United States (Massey and Denton 1993).

For the most part, the Civil Rights movement came quietly to South Florida, doing away with the formal institutions of segregation. But just at the point where new opportunities for upward mobility for Miami's Black minority began to occur, the city was transformed by the sudden arrival of Cuban refugees. In 1960, Black Americans greatly outnumbered Hispanics; by 1990 there were considerably more than twice as many Hispanics (987,394) as non-Hispanic Blacks (371,691) in Dade County. The demographic change was more than proportionately reflected in the economy, politics and culture.

In contrast to the Cuban American case, the quest by Black Miamians for political strength has confronted two debilitating conditions: weak community leadership and an unresponsive political system. The first was a by-product of typical 1960-era urban renewal programs, especially freeway construction. Urban renewal virtually destroyed Overtown, a vibrant center of small businesses and professionals serving the local Black population and culture. The result was the displacement of much of the Black middle class to newly desegregated suburbs, to new Black suburban developments such as Richmond Heights, or away from Miami altogether—often to southern cities, such as Atlanta, offering greater economic opportunity. Since Black communities are spread throughout the county and have no contiguous boundaries, it is much more difficult to develop common agendas and unified political action. In comparison, Hispanic communities are joined in a wide band extending westward from downtown Miami. The net result has been an early split between more affluent Black suburbs and an inner city Black underclass while Cuban American communities have managed to establish solid voting blocks throughout the county.

Similarly, Dade County's metropolitan governance system has contributed to the dilution of Black political power. It is argued that the movement to reform local politics in the late 1950s by developing the nation's first metropolitan government, including at-large elections for all commissioners, effectively squelched any effective forum for neighborhood and minority differences (Stack and Warren 1992, 163). At present, with some 60 percent of the area's Black population residing in unincorporated Dade County, and much of the remainder in the City of Miami with its large Hispanic majority, the chance of generating effective Black political representation is extremely low.

The combination of these fragmenting factors has been described as the "Miami Syndrome" (Stack and Warren 1992, 167)—a Black community divided by class, culture, and space which must function under double subordination to Anglos and Cubans. There's little wonder that effective leadership has been slow to develop and that the Cuban rise to the top has been accompanied by resentment and frustration.

The prospects for bridging these conflicts through coalitions are small. All Black legislators in Florida are Democrats; all Cuban American legislators are Republicans. This often elevates political conflicts to ethnic conflicts. For example, despite an initial flirtation around the possibility of a united stand on a minority reapportionment proposal, Black and Cuban legislators eventually clashed over the issue during the 1992 session of the Florida legislature. The current reapportionment battle promises to be just as contentious as the Republican controlled Legislature prepares to "design" the fate of the two Congressional seats gained in Florida after the 2000 Census, one of which will include portions of Miami-Dade County.

So, while the "Cuban Takeover" is not an absolute certainty, enough of it rings true to poison much of the ethnic waters in Miami-Dade County, particularly at the level of group perception.

Public Perceptions: A Widening Distance

When in 1993 a Cuban American woman was named to succeed Janet Reno as the state attorney for Dade County, thereby consolidating even more Cuban control of Miami's major institutions, a prominent Black leader was quoted to the effect that in Miami Hispanics are merely whites who speak Spanish. That is just one perception that African Americans hold of Cubans in Miami: that they are indistinguishable from the old "American" elite. Given the segregated nature of the two communities created by the completeness of the Cuban enclave, as well as their competition and ideological differences, is it not surprising that each holds stereotypical and hostile perceptions of each other which, in turn, contribute to deepen the original cleavages.

Grenier and Max Castro analyzed the content of the ethnic press from 1960 to 1992 and found that these perceptions have changed over time and not in a favorable direction. Analysis of editorials and interviews indicates the following pattern in the evolution of the Black/Latino relationship. During the 1960s and early 1970s Black Miami viewed Cubans as possible allies in the battles for minority empowerment in Dade County. The arrival of Cuban refugees was noted and commented upon in the Black press and on occasion sympathy for the plight of the refugees was expressed. Nevertheless, the major focus of the Black community was on issues associated with the classic civil rights struggles over desegregation, such as school integration.

While the level of Black attention to the Cuban refugee issue was limited, from the onset of large-scale Cuban immigration in the early 1960s concerns were voiced about possible adverse consequences for Blacks in jobs and preferential treatment of Cubans by local officials. As one indicator, editorials in the *Miami Times*, (Miami's Black newspaper of record, a weekly published since 1923) that mention Cubans critically increased in the 1970s. By the 1980s the initial view of sympathy or ambivalence was replaced by one of clear antagonism (Grenier and Castro, 1999).

In the Black press, the change to a harder line toward Cubans has extended even to some civil rights issues. As an example, in 1975 an editorial supported bilingualism and advised Blacks to learn Spanish; in 1980 the paper opposed the English only referendum as racist. By 1988, the paper advised its readers that conditions had changed. With Cubans now holding what was viewed as an oppressive power, the paper declined to oppose the Florida Official English Constitutional amendment.

Blacks view Puerto Ricans and Mexicans much more sympathetically. One African American civic leader interviewed characterized Puerto Ricans in Miami as "an invisible community," and described Blacks and Puerto Ricans as "natural allies" who nonetheless hardly ever worked together. Another African American political leader from the rural southern end of Miami-Dade, which contains the largest concentration of Mexicans, described Blacks and Mexicans as sharing similar cultural characteristics, while a Mexican American woman who works for a migrant advocacy organization in the same area stated that Blacks and Mexicans get along because of shared economic circumstances.

If the Black press increasingly reflects and reinforces an adversarial discourse toward Cubans, the Spanish-language daily press is marked by a seeming inattention or disinterest when it comes to the Black community. There is little evident concern in the Cuban community that the Black community could adversely affect its fate, except through riots that could damage Miami's image and economy.

However, there is a more covert Cuban discourse toward Blacks, and it emerges more clearly in other media and channels: in the pages of tabloids and newsletters, on radio talk shows, and in daily conversations and interactions. The elements of this discourse include the denial of racism and of any responsibility in redressing its toll, identification of Blacks with crime, strong support for police, and an invidious comparison between Cuban economic advancement through hard work, family and self reliance, and Black dependency on welfare and other social programs. Illustrative of the covert nature of some of this discourse, as well as its major themes, is *Hispanews,* an unsigned 1993 newsletter issued by a previously unknown group, the Federation of Hispanic Employees of Dade County. One passage, a response to an editorial in the *Miami Times* accusing Cubans of insensitivity to Blacks, brings together denial of racism and invidious comparison:

> Under this label [insensitivity], the newspaper launches against Cubans the variety of rockets usually reserved for Anglos. Our answer is that it may be okay with Anglos, since, historically, they are guilty of enslaving and degrading Blacks for centuries; they owe Blacks. But, folks, we Hispanics owe Blacks nothing: what are we guilty of? Of hard work, not only as bankers and entrepreneurs, but also as humble laborers and peddlers? Keep it clear in your head that we have never coerced assistance from anyone, but much rather roam the streets of Miami selling limes, onions, flowers, peanuts, etc. Some folks should try this, it is hard work, but not bad.

A Case in Point: The Mandela Incident and the Tourism Boycott

The triadic ethnic structure of Miami—Black, Latino, Anglo—often underlies and confounds the apparently dyadic Black/Cuban relationship. In the case of Blacks, who are in the weakest position structurally, there is evidence from interviews that some Black leaders self-consciously attempt to employ a pragmatic strategy of shifting alliances to maximize Black influence.

An illustrative incident originated in the treatment Nelson Mandela received when he visited Miami in 1990. Unlike the civic honors bestowed at his other stops, the official Miami reception was decidedly cool, the product of Cuban (and, to a lesser extent, Jewish) outrage at his refusal to disavow Fidel Castro and Yasser Arafat. The mayors of Miami Beach and Miami, as well as the Miami-Dade Commission, refused to honor or meet with Mandela, much to the anger of local Black leaders. Most Black elected officials did not take a stand on this issue, perhaps an example of the divisiveness sometimes arising within the Black community, in this case directly related to fears about Cuban political retaliation.

About a week after the Mandela visit, a local fight between a Cuban proprietor and a Haitian customer in a Little Haiti store resulted in a public disturbance. Dozens of Haitians demonstrated in front of the small store, requiring police intervention and resulting in charges of police brutality. That same week, a group of Black professionals and community leaders, including the Black Lawyers' Association, headed by H. T. Smith, organized a boycott, calling on national organizations with conventions scheduled in Miami to take their business elsewhere. The demands of the Boycott Coalition were an apology to Nelson Mandela from Miami's elected officials, an investigation into police conduct in the Haitian demonstration, a series of economic measures to promote Black economic interests, especially in the tourist industry, and the reform of Miami's political system to provide greater Black representation.

The boycott had an impact. Before the end of 1990, thirteen organizations, including the American Civil Liberties Union and the National Organization of Women, had canceled Miami conferences. In all, Miami is estimated to have lost over $60 million in convention-related business. After lengthy negotiations between Anglo economic elites and Black boycott leaders, talks which purposefully excluded Cubans, a settlement was reached. The Greater Miami Convention and Visitors Bureau, with local corporate sponsorship, eventually established a scholarship program at Florida International University for Black students to receive training and subsequent management level employment in the local tourist industry. The Miami Beach Commission agreed to promote the development of a new Black-owned hotel. The Mayor of Miami Beach and the Miami-Dade Commission issued retroactive statements honoring Mandela, while the Cuban American mayor of the City of Miami admitted the situation may not have been handled well. The boycott was lifted in 1993.

The issue seemingly at the heart of the boycott—the city fathers' failure to honor Nelson Mandela—was an ideological one that pitted Cubans against Blacks. But the real goal of the boycott, as later developments and the statements of the boycott leader showed, was to wrest economic concessions from the Anglo corporate elite. The Mandela issue, according to the principal boycott organizer, was gladly seized upon as a symbolic rallying point to mobilize the community, enlist outside solidarity, and dramatize the plight of Blacks in Miami. In this case, a Black/Hispanic dispute was capitalized upon in order to inspire a boycott aimed at the local white establishment.

Elements of Cooperation

Within the context of a generally adversarial relationship, there are instances, areas, and possibilities of common action and empathy. In 1992, a fragile Black/Hispanic coalition successfully sued Metropolitan Dade County, overturning the at-large voting system that had kept Black and Hispanic participation to a single member each in a nine-member commission. Following the establishment of thirteen districts, the next election resulted in a new Metropolitan Dade County Commission composed of four African Americans (including the Chair), six Hispanics, and three Anglos. This restructuring enhances Black representation in the politics of the region. South Florida currently has two African Americans, Carrie Meeks and Alcee Hastings, serving in the U.S. Congress and six African American state legislators. Blacks serve on the current city commissions or councils of Miami, El Portal, Opa Locka, and Florida City—the latter two predominantly Black communities also have Black mayors (Metro-Dade County 1994).

Similarly, in the Spring of 1993, after lengthy discussions with leaders of the Spanish American League Against Discrimination, the Miami-Dade branch of the NAACP supported a successful attempt to abolish the county's English only ordinance, which Hispanics had vehemently opposed. The NAACP cited, along with other reasons of principle, the adverse impact of the ordinance on the large Creole-speaking Miami Haitian community. The four Black county commissioners voted for repeal of English Only.

There have been other sporadic instances of cooperation. The visible support by the more politically moderate Cuban leaders for restoration of Haitian democracy and against deportation of Haitians has brought some Black and Cuban leaders ephemerally together and helped assuage, at least momentarily, resentment over disparate treatment of Cuban versus Haitian refugees. When Cuban American pop star Gloria Estefan gave a benefit concert in March 1992, the United Negro College Fund was one of four charities to receive the proceeds. Earlier, Black lawyers and their Cuban American counterparts together organized a fundraising ball. An organization of Black Cubans formed in the 1990s has attempted to serve as a bridge between white Cubans and African Americans, with limited success.

Efforts to improve Black/Cuban relations continue. The Community Relations Board of Miami-Dade County government, a tri-ethnic committee which conducts activities designed to develop joint agendas, initiated a Maceo/King Initiative bringing together the Cuban Civic Council and the NAACP. Named after a Black Cuban independence war hero, Antonio Maceo, and the Black civil rights leader, the program seeks to facilitate join ventures and business partnerships between Cuban and African Americans in South Florida.

CONCLUSION

While the Cuban community has prospered under the guidance of the established American white community, Miami's African American community feels left behind. Although many African Americans have advanced into professional and executive positions since the arrival of Cubans, the majority remain poor and feel culturally marginalized. Equally important, in spite of the lack of evidence, many blame the Cubans for the relative failure of African Americans. Ethnic tensions in Miami are extreme, seething constantly and fuming periodically. The contrast between Miami's Cuban and African American communities discloses the coincidental fortuitousness of the Cuban success—immigration created by a Cold War confrontation that produced an abundant welcome, including massive state aid; settlement in a city geographically perfect and poised for a new role as a nexus to Latin America; a profile of immigrants that began with an early upward social and economic selectivity that was followed by controlled and limited waves of working class immigrants; and internal right-wing hegemony that produced extraordinarily high community trust and internal cooperation for those who submitted to the dominant ideology. The absence of any one of these factors easily could have changed the entire profile of the community, and, perhaps, its relations with other ethnic groups.

The diversity of the ethnic groups in Miami continues to increase. As it stands, Miami-Dade County is the most populous majority minority metropolitan area in the United States. Latinos comprise 57 percent of the population and Blacks, including African Americans and immigrant Blacks, make up 20 percent. Non-Hispanic whites make up 21 percent of the shrinking balance. And while Cubans and African Americans are now the dominant groups within the Latino and Black community, the 2000 Census makes clear the diversification trend. Mexicans newcomers have increased their numbers by 65 percent, Columbians by 31 percent and Puerto Ricans by 10 percent. Similarly, immigrants from the West Indies, including Haitians and Jamaicans, have increased by 117 percent from 1990, bringing their numbers (500,000) close to the 651,000 of the Cubans and adding another newcomer Black voice to the ethnic choir.

Some of these newcomers will benefit from the political and economic strength of the Cuban community, as have Nicaraguans and middle-class Colombians. Others will feel marginalized and excluded from its success, as some say Mexicans and Haitians do. Cubans, for their part, will need to see the necessity to make bridges and create alliances with the diverse communities. Cubans have not done this often enough, in the opinion of many. As an African American writer for *The Miami Herald* notes:

> Since emerging as a significant presence here, Cubans have not particularly needed allies. They've prospered, placing their cultural and political stamp on Miami-Dade County

largely by using their own resources and determination. In addition, many have set the bar of friendship too high for most non-Cubans to reach.... Many older Cubans view non-Cubans as irrelevant to their lives (Steinback 2001).

For the time being, developing harmonious Black/Latino relations in Miami remains an enormous challenge, for the main Black and Latino communities are divided by space, class, party, ideology, language, and religion. The task ahead for leaders and citizens is to show how such a divisions can be overcome under the most difficult of circumstances.

7

Political Culture

The Exile Ideology and Electoral Politics

On October 18, 1997, a young Cuban pitcher named Liván Hernández threw a strike to Cleveland Indians infielder Bip Roberts to start the opening game of the World Series. Hernández went on to win the game for the Florida Marlins, to the cheers of more than 60,000 fans (including many Cuban Americans waving Cuban flags) gathered at Pro Player Stadium, just north of Miami.

A few years before, when Liván was still pitching for the Cuban national baseball team, the mayor of the small city of Homestead, Florida, just south of Greater Miami, succeeded in attracting to his city a portion of the games scheduled for an international amateur baseball tournament being played in various cities throughout the United States. The mayor (who is not of Cuban origin) did not have a large Cuban American constituency, but he knew that the largest concentration of Cubans in the United States was located just a short drive away and that they always seemed to be interested in their native country. As a gesture of neighborly goodwill, and no doubt with an interest in attracting large crowds to Homestead's brand-new baseball stadium, he arranged to have the Cuban national baseball team included among those scheduled to play in his city.

As soon as the news reached Miami's Cubans that Homestead would be hosting the Cuban team, the mayor found himself vilified by the Spanish-language radio stations in Miami and no less than a member of the U.S. Congress labeled his actions as grossly insensitive and offensive to his Cuban American neighbors. Faced with such a reaction, the vexed and perplexed mayor quickly had the game schedule rearranged so that Homestead would not host the Cuban team. He was therefore disabused of what seemed a perfectly sensible, yet evidently mistaken, assumption: that a community of Cuban Americans would welcome the Cuban national baseball team.

The incident is one example of how the political behavior of Cuban Americans is frequently difficult to understand and appears to defy reason. Moreover, things are not always what they appear to be. For example, consider what might have happened if the mayor had not changed his mind about hosting the Cuban team. He would have faced a crescendo of opposition from the Cuban American community, including calls for a boycott of the game, demonstrations, and threats of violence. However, he also would have been surprised to encounter some Cuban American support for going ahead with the game and to find that his original expectation regarding a good turnout by Cuban Americans was not entirely off the mark. In other words, the mayor would have learned that the political culture of Cuban Americans is a complex one, fraught with strong emotions, contradictions, and nuances that make it perplexing and difficult to understand and appreciate in all its dimensions. Or, to put it in the vernacular, he probably would have concluded that he couldn't figure out those Cubans.

That conclusion would have been further reinforced in the mayor's mind had he been one of the fans at Pro Player Stadium during Hernández's win over the Indians. How was it possible that not long before Hernández and his teammates were not welcomed to Homestead by their compatriots, while now all these Cuban Americans were cheering wildly for Hernández in the World Series? Go figure.

Such apparent contradictions are not, of course, limited to baseball. One of the biggest contradictions is in the crucial area of the relationship between Cuban Americans and their homeland. On the one hand, pressure and lobbying from Cuban American leaders and organizations have been a critical factor in maintaining a hostile U.S. policy intended to economically isolate Cuba. On the other hand, remittances and visits from Cuban Americans to the island are estimated to amount to as much as $800 million each year, surpassing what the island earns from tourism and not far behind its income from sales in the international sugar market. Again, go figure.

That is precisely the purpose of this chapter, to attempt to "figure out," or make understandable, what is most puzzling and contradictory about Cuban Americans: their political culture. The core of that culture is the exile ideology, and most of this chapter deals with defining that ideology, its manifestations, and its implications.

THE PERSISTENCE OF THE EXILE IDEOLOGY

Whatever image most Americans have of Cuban Americans is probably constituted, more than anything else, by these political traits: staunch anti-Castroism, militancy, conservatism, and affiliation with the Republican Party. These assumed political features of the community result from and reinforce the one characteristic that gives the community its identity: an obsession with the past, present and future of Cuba. Anti-Castroism might well be considered to be the master status of the community, establishing the limits and potentials for all group activity. In that sense, the community is assumed to be frozen in time. One would think that after forty years some things would have changed. But when studying Cubans in the United States, and especially in Miami, one often has to explain why some things have not changed. The persistence of an exile ideology is an important part of the apparent immutability of the community.

The forging and maintenance of the exile identity have contributed to the creation of a particularly "Cuban" way of looking at the social and political environment. We refer to this vision of the world as "the exile ideology." In many ways, this world view differentiates Cubans from non-Cubans in Miami and in the rest of the country. As we shall see, not all Cubans in the United States share this ideology, but it is a critical reference point that serves to define the identity of Cuban Americans. The exile ideology is a basic ingredient in the development of a "moral community" that serves to build political capital and a sense of solidarity in the enclave, as discussed in Chapter 3.

The exile ideology has three principal and interrelated characteristics: (1) the primacy of the homeland; (2) uncompromising hostility towards the Castro government; and (3) emotionalism, irrationality, and intolerance.

The Primacy of the Homeland

During one week in the summer of 1984, the English-language press in Miami was warning residents of Little Havana to take precautions because the state of Florida was about to thoroughly spray them, from the air, with a chemical that might inflict damage to, among other things, car finishes. It seems an insect harmful to citrus trees was found in the area. However, in the Spanish-language radio and press, the media most followed in Little Havana, there was scant mention of the impending fumigation. All the attention, most of it negative, was focused on the visit of the Rev. Jesse Jackson to Havana and the possibility that the Cuban government would release political prisoners. Even as they were being sprayed from above, the news from the island was evidently far more important to Cubans than such mundane local concerns as exposure to a harmful chemical.

In the exile ideology, the affairs of the homeland represent the community's foremost priority. The public discourse is largely preoccupied with the political status of the homeland. A key element of any exile consciousness is the fact that the members of the community were forced out of their country; emigration was not a choice, as with so many other immigrants, but a survival strategy allowing them to live and fight another day. Emigration is part of an enduring conflict. During the past forty years there has been a protracted continuation of the intense conflict that occurred from about 1960 to 1962, when the Cuban regime was entrenching itself against the serious attempts by the U.S. government and various sectors of Cuban society to overthrow it. For many Cubans who "lost" that conflict and went into exile, the struggle has not ended, and they have tried, with amazing success, to keep the conflict alive.

The desire to recover the homeland shapes the behavior of the exiles in the host country. It is the focus of political discourse and the source of mobilization in the Cuban American community. U.S. policy towards Cuba and the internal situation in the island continue to predominate. In contrast, a certain apathy characterizes the attitude towards more domestic issues, such as the adoption of English as the official language of Florida.

The importance of Cuba for the Cuban American community is often ridiculed since Cuba is often seen as central to issues that seem far removed from foreign policy matters, at least to the general public. For example, Miami-Dade County was the only county in the country with an ordinance preventing county funds from being used in any business activity involving Cuban nationals. In most situations, this prohibition was redundant given the federal trade sanctions currently in place, but the ordinance had a direct impact on local cultural organizations working within the legal limits of the federal trade sanctions. Organizations promoting cultural exchanges, musical or in the plastic arts, faced the prospect of having their county funds suspended or at least publicly scrutinized if Cuban artists were involved in local activities. Although the ordinance was judged unconstitutional in 2000, support for it did not go away. When asked in the FIU Cuba Poll 2000 if they supported the principles of the revoked ordinance, 49 percent of Cuban Americans in Miami-Dade said that they did, as compared to 25 percent of non-Cubans.

This obsession with Cuba spills over into the political process in another way. Many Cuban Americans use the Cuba issue as a litmus test for evaluating candidates for local office. "If you want to run for dog catcher," said a Cuban American patron at a sidewalk coffee stand, "you'd better take a hardline position towards Cuba or you'll never get elected." While it may not be that extreme, it is true that Miami politics dances to a Cuban beat. Indeed, in the Cuban Poll 2000 question measuring the salience of Cuba on local politics, 77 percent of Miami Cuban Americans said that a candidate's position on Cuba was important in determining their vote. As you might expect, this contrasted sharply with non-Cubans both at the local and national level.

The primacy of the homeland explains the overwhelming preference for the Republican Party, a trait that sets Cubans apart from other Latino groups. Registered Republicans far outnumbered registered Democrats among Cubans in Miami in the year 2000, to the tune of approximately 67 percent Republicans and 17 percent Democrats. In the mind of a typical Cuban American, loyalty to the Republican Party demonstrates the importance of international issues in the political agenda of Cubans. If a substantial number in the Cuban community disagreed with elements of the exile ideology, or if there was a greater balance in that agenda, with importance given to purely domestic issues, the Democratic Party would have made greater inroads.

In fact, if Cuban Americans were to view themselves as immigrants in this country, rather than as political exiles, and made judgments about political parties based upon their needs and aspirations as immigrants in the United States, they would be Democrats in overwhelming numbers. This would be true not only because of the general social agenda of the Democrats but also because of the specific experience of Cuban migration. The measures that have greatly facilitated Cuban immigration and the adjustment of Cuban Americans in the United States have all been enacted by Democratic administrations: the Cuban Refugee Emergency Program and its resettlement efforts, the assistance given to the Cuban elderly and the dependent, the establishment of the Airlift or Freedom Flights, and permission for the Mariel boatlift to take place, among others.

The fact that Cubans are overwhelmingly Republican is therefore a testimony to the importance of homeland issues and the perception that Republicans are more in tune with the anti-Castro agenda. It is interesting to note, however, that the Cuban American delegation in the Florida state legislature in Tallahassee has shown an ambivalence to supporting the party to which most of their constituency belongs. Strongly influenced by the Cuban labor leadership, this group is viewed as a liberal force within the Republican Party and often enters into coalition with Democrats to impede the domination of the state legislature by conservative Republicans or Democrats.

Uncompromising Hostility Towards the Castro Government

The goal of the Cuban exile is the overthrow of Fidel Castro. This is to be accomplished through hostility and isolation, not rapprochement. Such an ideology has, in general terms, been consistent with United States policy towards Cuba over the past forty years. In fact, it is generally accepted that pressure from Cuban Americans has been the major factor keeping U.S. Cuba policy essentially immutable for four decades and focused on a strategy of isolating Cuba.

Cuban Americans did not begin to exert a significant influence on the U.S. Cuba policy until after 1980. Prior to that time, the establishment and continuation of a hostile policy towards Cuba resided exclusively in Washington, with exiles playing a merely supportive role, as exemplified by the failed 1961 Bay of Pigs invasion. U.S. administrations in the 1960s and 1970s adhered to the principle that the United States does not reestablish relations or grant diplomatic recognition to what it regards as hostile or rogue regimes. Cuba had not only wiped out the overwhelming U.S. economic and political presence on the island, but, at the height of the Cold War, it had switched to Moscow's side and continued, in Washington's eyes, to behave badly, especially in attempting to export its revolution to Latin America. In that context, both Republican and Democratic administrations had absolutely no basis or motivation to alter the outlines of the policy established by Eisenhower and Kennedy and end the isolation and embargo of Cuba—far from it. Throughout the 1960s there were even U.S.-sponsored attempts to destabilize the Castro government, many using Cuban exiles as operatives.

Until 1980, it was therefore Washington, waging a Cold War and intent on punishing and destabilizing the government in Havana for its misdeeds, that carried the ball in pursuing the policy of hostility and isolation. Starting in 1980, however, a new set of forces and actors comes into play to help maintain, and even reinforce, that long-standing policy. It was the year that marked the beginning of a shift in the role of Cuban exiles from mere agents or implementers of U.S. policy to major players in Washington's actions towards Cuba.

The catalyst for the shift was the presidential election of 1980. The candidacy and election of Ronald Reagan had two consequences: it dramatically increased the participation of Cuban Americans in the U.S. electoral system and it prompted the formation of an exile lobby group in Washington. Up until that year, many Cubans in the United States, especially the elderly, had been slow to apply for U.S. citizenship and register to vote, despite having long met the necessary requirements to do so. This reluctance was based on the persistence of an exile ideology, which led them to reject an assimilative immigrant mentality. The Reagan candidacy, however, made participation in the U.S. electoral system consistent with the exile agenda of recovering the homeland. The Republican candidate was viewed as an ideologically-committed anti-communist who would be really tough on Castro. Becoming U.S. citizens and voting in November, far from being an indication of assimilation in the United States, was actually a strategy within the traditional exile agenda.

The surge in 1980 in Cuban American voting strength created, by the mid-to-late 1980s, considerable forces against softening the U.S. Cuba policy. One such force was the creation of a noticeable Cuban

American voting bloc in Florida and, to a lesser extent, in New Jersey, both key electoral states. Politicians quickly learned, correctly, that those blocs were easily swayed by supporting a hard-line policy against the Cuban government. That tactic has been widely used by Congressional as well as Presidential candidates, and by both Republicans and Democrats. A related development was the election, starting in the late 1980s, of Cuban Americans to Congress. Numbering three at present, the Cuban Americans Congressmen have placed a priority on maintaining and strengthening current policy towards Cuba, thereby forming a committed core of members within Congress working to keep that policy from changing.

The election of Ronald Reagan created the conditions for the development of yet another important vehicle for exiles to capture the direction of U.S. policy towards Cuba. By 1980, a successful entrepreneurial class with accumulated surplus capital had emerged within the Cuban American community. This new prosperity could be tapped to create a presence in Washington to further the anti-Castro agenda, and the election of a president perceived as friendly to that cause seemed a propitious moment for such a step. This convergence of economic and political conditions made possible the creation of the Cuban American National Foundation (CANF).

The CANF followed the traditional formula of legitimate U.S. interest groups: campaign contributions, political fundraisers, lobbying, information dissemination, media relations, etc. It was anti-Castroism "the American way." With offices in Washington and Miami, the CANF occupied during the 1980s and into the early 1990s the center stage in the Cuban American community's struggle against the Cuban government. It became the major protagonist in the exiles' increasing role in determining U.S. policy toward Cuba.

CANF members have been typically successful businesspeople who have made their wealth in the United States and given thousands of dollars annually to further the organization's work. Their focus on lobbying in Washington places their strategy within the context of U.S./Cuba relations, with the goal of overthrowing the Castro government through a policy of hostility and isolation spearheaded by the United States. The CANF played a critical role in the passage of both the 1992 Cuban Democracy Act (the "Torricelli Act") and the 1996 Cuban Liberty and Democratic Solidarity (Libertad) Act (the "Helms-Burton Act"), both of which tightened the U.S. embargo on Cuba. It was largely responsible for the establishment by the U.S. government of Radio and TV Martí, which broadcasts to Cuba.

By the 1980s, therefore, Cuban exiles had become major players in sustaining and strengthening the policy that the United States had established toward the island. Their increasing influence in the 1980s and 1990s, through the ballot box, representation in Congress, and lobbying, constitute the principal force for inertia in that policy of hostility.

Hard-line attitudes toward the anti-Castro struggle prevail within the community. The FIU Cuba Poll 2000 found that over 60 percent of the Cuban American population in Miami still favors military action against the Cuban government, either by the United States or by exile groups. The military option is not far from the minds of many hard-liners. After the February 1996 crisis initiated by the downing of two Cuban American Cessnas over the Straits of Florida by Cuban Air Force pilots, the majority of Miami Cubans did not hesitate in calling for a United States invasion of the island. Such events strengthen the hand of the hard-liners, in Miami as well as in Cuba.

Support for trade sanctions against the island, the embargo, is another element of the incessant struggle against the Cuban government. The fact that forty years of trade sanctions have not brought about a change in the government does not go unnoticed. Over 74 percent of Miami Cuban Americans are aware that the embargo has not worked, yet 62 percent favor its continuation.

Emotionalism, Irrationality, and Intolerance

Support for the embargo underscores yet another trait of the political culture of Cubans in the United States: the importance of emotion over pragmatism. While admitting that the embargo may be ineffective, and, further, even recognizing that lifting it may well bring about significant changes in Cuba, a majority in the Cuban community continue to oppose any such softening of U.S. policy because of its symbolism. If the United States abandons its hard-line stance against Cuba, the argument goes, Fidel Castro will have "won" the forty-year struggle. It is therefore a struggle that is based not so much on pragmatism as it is on emotion.

The Cuban American community has been formed by a particular set of political circumstances. Those circumstances have had a great personal impact on members of the community. Cuban Americans—as with exiles everywhere—are therefore not likely to be objective about the situation that has so intrinsically altered their lives and compelled them to live outside their native country. The emotional basis of the exile ideology is what makes Cubans in the United States take positions that others judge to be irrational, as happened in the case of Elián González (see Chapter 8). Of course, many Cuban exiles will readily, and even proudly, admit to not being rational in matters that have touched them so deeply, and will even flaunt their passionate lack of objectivity. One participant in a Miami demonstration carried a placard that read: *Intransigente...¿y qué?* (Intransigent...so what?).

Energizing the emotionalism of the community is the highly personalized nature of the anti-Castro struggle. The enduring presence in Cuba of the historical leader of its socialist revolution is a key factor in maintaining distance and hostility between Cuban exiles and the government in Cuba. For most Cubans in the United States, the culprit responsible for their exile is not a political movement, not a revolution, not a government, but a person. Fidel Castro represents a continuation of a long-standing Cuban tradition in which authority has a primarily personal, not institutional, base. In this case, of course, it is not a perception divorced from reality.

The least favorable side of emotionalism and irrationality is a traditional intolerance to views that do not conform to the predominant "exile" ideology of an uncompromising hostility towards the Castro regime. Those inside or outside the community who voice views that are "soft" or conciliatory with respect to Castro, or who take a less-than-militant stance in opposition to Cuba's regime, are usually subjected to criticism and scorn, their position belittled and their motives questioned. Liberals, the "liberal press", most Democrats, pacifists, leftists, academics, intellectuals, "dialoguers," and socialists are favorite targets. Any dissent within the community is especially difficult, since great pressure can be brought to bear on the individual or group. Moreover, intolerance of opposing views has frequently been a source of friction between Cubans and other groups and institutions in Miami. The exiles' inflexible anti-Castroism has frequently been criticized—and even ridiculed—by non-Cubans in Miami, especially when it manifests itself as attempts to censor cultural events in Miami by artists or intellectuals from Cuba.

Cuban Americans are aware of the forces of censorship in the community but are not often sensitive to them. For years we asked our poll respondents if they felt that all views towards Cuba were being heard in the community. Not surprisingly, a sizable majority would always respond that, no, not all views were being heard. In the Cuba Poll 2000 we inserted a follow-up question which asked specifically about the views that they felt were being suppressed. The answers were surprising. Of the 79 percent who felt that not all views were being heard, over 50 percent felt that voices of stronger opposition to the Castro regime are suppressed!

CURRENTS OF CHANGE

Although the exile ideology persists and dominates, not all Cuban Americans can be painted with the same brush. The fact is that Cuban

Americans are a diverse population or at least not the political monolith so often portrayed.

Departures from the traditional exile ideology began to manifest themselves at the end of the Cold War. With the fall of the Berlin Wall, Cuban exiles who had long struggled to overthrow an entrenched socialist regime now had in Eastern Europe an operational model of how such a thing might be accomplished. Rather than an overnight "rupture" scenario traditionally envisioned by the exiles, the new model involved an evolution that might be led by elements from within "the system," a process that could be helped by openness rather than hostility and isolation. Consequently, some Cuban Americans, including some traditional hard-liners, began to espouse a strategy of promoting a relaxation of tensions with Havana and engaging elements within Cuba. The rise of this new orientation led in the 1990s to the establishment of several organizations that, in different ways, conceptualized anti-Castro activism in more moderate terms, espousing an elimination of hostility and emphasizing constructive relations with the Cuban government. These new organizations have been committed to a peaceful transition to democracy that would not be based on confrontation and hostility.

These developments served to broaden the ideological spectrum of Cuban exile politics, creating new voices that argued against a continuation of the current U.S. policy. Although these new elements have thus far failed to gain predominance within the community, they have served to challenge what had been a monolithic image of exile politics, providing support for initiatives that challenge the traditional course of U.S./Cuba relations.

In addition to the rise of moderate political voices and organizations, perhaps an even greater challenge to the continuation of a policy of isolation towards Cuba has developed within the exile community. Cuban Americans whose only motivation is to visit and help family and friends on the island represent a major point of contact between the two countries. Remittances and family visits provide Cuba with more foreign exchange than its tourism industry and fuel the development of a more moderate voice within the Miami community.

The 1994 and 1995 migration accords between the United States and Cuba raised the ceiling for Cuban migration to the United States. Since then, some 20,000 Cubans have come to the United States each year in an authorized fashion, in addition to the smaller number who arrive through unauthorized means. This new influx, added to those who came during and after Mariel, serves to increase the number of Cubans in the United States with an interest in sending remittances and returning to visit relatives. Unlike the earlier migration wave that departed at the height of the Cold War and have sought to keep the anti-Castro struggle alive, newer arrivals are likely to place priority on communicating with their families still in Cuba. The earlier exiles are much less likely to have maintained family ties in the island.

The FIU Cuba Poll has consistently shown that the most recent arrivals to the United States tend to have the most moderate views on how to deal with the island. For example, a majority (54 percent) of those arriving after 1984 favor lifting the embargo. Among those arriving in the 1960s and 1970s, less than a third favored lifting it.

In addition to the new arrivals, two other important sectors of the Cuban population of the United States tend to add diversity to the political culture: the new generations and those living outside of Miami. The FIU poll shows that members of the second generation (born in the United States) are much more conciliatory in their views towards island politics than their parents. The same is true of Cubans who do not live within the insularity of the Miami enclave and are therefore less likely to have maintained an exile ideology. According to the 1995 poll, Cubans living in New Jersey are more likely to favor a dialogue with the Castro regime than those living in Miami. Similarly, New Jersey Cubans are less likely to be influenced by a candidate's position on Cuba as they cast their vote in local and national elections. As the process of concentration in South Florida continues, the arrival in Miami of Cubans who have lived elsewhere in the United States adds yet another source of pluralism to the political landscape.

All of these forces for political diversity were evident by the time of the FIU Cuba Poll 2000. The poll showed that 51 percent of Miami Cubans favored a dialogue with the Cuban government and anywhere from 33 to 39 percent would like to lift the embargo. A much higher percentage would like to lift restrictions on food (56 percent) and medicine (66 percent) exports to the island. These figures show that even on issues that tend to define Cuban Americans to the world, the community is much more pluralistic than often thought.

PARTICIPATION IN THE U.S. POLITICAL SYSTEM

In the fall of 1990, Arthur Teele got to know Little Havana very well. Teele, an African American Republican who had made his name as a functionary in Reagan's Department of Transportation, was running for county commissioner. His opponent, the incumbent commissioner Barbara Carey, was well known and respected in the Black community. Teele did the numbers and decided that his best chance to win the at-large seat was by focusing on the Cuban community. He said as much: "[W]e felt that the only place that we could not beat Commissioner Carey was in the Black community. She put most of her resources in one place and I didn't" (Feldstein Soto 1990). He made the rounds of the Cuban organizations, the restaurants, and the elderly activities centers known as *comedores,* courting Cubans, most of whom are registered Republicans and who have a sterling record of turning out to vote. He was particularly welcomed in the *comedores* where the elderly Latinos were pleased to have Teele recognize their importance. The *comedores* were important to Teele because they provide transportation to the voting booth. In a close race, these several thousand votes could be essential.

The strategy paid off. Teele won the election, receiving two of every three Cuban votes while losing four out of every five votes from the Black community. He became the Black community's representative on the commission without receiving the majority of the Black vote.

Fast forward to 1996. Teele is running again after serving five successful years as a commissioner. This time he is aiming to become the first strong mayor of Miami-Dade County, a newly created office replacing the weak mayor system which was a result of the 1960 "good government" restructuring of the county. His opponent this time around is Alex Penelas, who entered county government as a commissioner along with Teele in 1990. At that time, Penelas ran a campaign which emphasized his Cubanness. He had to. His opponent for the 1990 commission seat, Jorge Valdés, was an old guard Cuban who made ethnic purity a major theme of his campaign. Valdés mocked Penelas as a "Cuban wannabe" saying that it takes more than eating chicken and rice in a Calle Ocho restaurant to be a real Cuban. Penelas, young and of Cuban parentage, but born in Hialeah, feebly fought back defending his Cubanness. At one point his mother appealed to the public during a popular Cuban radio talk show, saying, "It's not his fault that he was born in this country."

Penelas won, but split the Cuban vote. Had it not been for the white Anglo vote, he might not have had the opportunity to run in the 1996 race where he faced Teele for control of the largest metropolitan area in the fourth largest state in the union.

In 1996, both candidates returned to their ethnic roots. Teele, though still a Republican, had built a solid record of addressing the concerns of the African American community and had gained the respect of many of its civic leaders. For his part, Penelas had become the darling of the Cuban American community, a young rising star whose political future some saw leading to the governor's mansion. While discussion and debates on his record and experience were heard, the bottom line to many voters was ethnicity. Penelas was the Cuban candidate, Teele the African American candidate. Each community was expected to support its own. They did.

Both the Hispanic and Black communities mobilized forces. The result of the 1996 election was significant because of the polarization of the communities along ethnic lines. Penelas garnered a little over 60

Arthur Teele (left) and Alex Penelas debate during the 1996 campaign for Miami-Dade County mayor.

(The Miami Herald/Nuri Vallbona)

percent of the votes and an estimated 80 percent of the Hispanic vote but only 3 percent of the Black vote. The numbers for Teele were the mirror image of these. His overwhelming 84 percent support by the African American community was not enough to push him to victory (with the two percent of the Hispanic vote). "Even when African Americans turn out," remarked a Teele campaign worker, "we can't put one of ours in office."

These two elections, years apart, show the significance of the Cuban American population in local politics. Cuban Americans are now the driving force behind the electoral trends in Miami-Dade County. The importance of the Cuban American vote, which Arthur Teele first recognized in 1990, continues to be reinforced in recent elections and received empirical verification on November 5, 1996. On that day, Dade's total electorate reached 849,046 registered voters, and 39 percent of those voters were Hispanic, making Latinos the largest voting bloc in the county. White non-Hispanics made up 38 percent of the electorate. Black non-Hispanic voters were 20 percent. The Cuban voting bloc has to be considered by any candidate seeking county-wide office.

The influence Cuban Americans exert over elections in South Florida was not achieved overnight. As noted previously, the starting point was the candidacy of Ronald Reagan. The ideology of the Republican candidate on foreign policy was appealing to many Cubans, and it served to link exile politics with registration and voting in the United States. Participation in the U.S. political system, therefore, was actually an extension of exile concerns (de la Garza et al. 1994).

During the 1980s, Cubans in Miami established pivotal local power, exercised through the increasing number of elected officials and such organizations as the Cuban American National Foundation, the Latin Builders Association and the Hispanic Builders Association, and the Latin Chamber of Commerce. The size of the Cuban community in Greater Miami and its fairly high turnout rates during elections produced a boom in the number of Cubans in elected positions at all levels of government. By the late 1980s, the City of Miami had a Cuban-born mayor, and the city manager and the county manager were both Cubans. Cubans controlled the City Commission and constituted more than one-third of the Dade delegation to the state legislature. After Claude Pepper died, a Cuban, Ileana Ros-Lehtinen, won his U.S. House of Representatives seat in 1989.

By the 1990s Cuban Americans were mayors of the incorporated areas of Miami, Hialeah, Sweetwater, West Miami, and Hialeah Gardens, all within Greater Miami-Dade. Cubans comprised a majority in the commissions or councils of those cities. When the 1990s began there were already ten Cubans in the Florida Legislature, seven in the House and three in the Senate. Ileana Ros-Lehtinen was joined by another Cuban, Lincoln Diaz-Balart, in the U.S. Congress during the 1992 election cycle. By the beginning of the twenty-first century, six of the thirteen Miami-Dade County commissioners are Cuban as is the mayor, Alex Penelas. Nowhere else in America, nor even in American history, have first generation immigrants so quickly, or so thoroughly, appropriated political power.

CONCLUSION

There are two contrasting stories in this chapter. The first one is the story of Cubans as exiles and of the ideology that has led them at times to behave in ways that the rest of the country finds unreasonable and even irrational. It is the story of the relentless and enduring pursuit of the exile goal of recovering the homeland by triumphing over the regime, or more accurately, the person, who is responsible for their exile. That pursuit has frequently led to unfortunate episodes and behaviors, most evident during the Elián González saga, in which Cuban Americans were heavily criticized and viewed with derision and ridiculed by many non-Cubans in Miami and throughout the nation. It is a story of frustration, misunderstandings, and resentment.

The other story is one of achievement and victories. It is the story of an immigrant group that has made unprecedented gains in empowering themselves in the new country. The successes achieved through the ballot box, detailed in this chapter, have been matched by their economic achievements: the creation of a solid ethnic enclave with strong social capital that facilitates economic adjustment. These achievements have earned praise and respect from others and have created a positive image of Cuban Americans as strong entrepreneurs with extraordinary political influence in South Florida.

The contrast of the two stories is ironic. The core of the identity of Cubans in the United States is as exiles, not immigrants. If the goal of exiles is to recover the homeland, and the job of immigrants is to successfully adjust economically and empower themselves in the new country, then we can reach the conclusion first formulated by our colleague Max Castro: Cubans in the United States have been a failure at what they say they are, and a success at what they say they are not.

8

The Trophy

Elián González and the Cuban American Community

On Thanksgiving Day, 1999, a six-year-old boy was found floating on an inner tube three miles off the Florida coast. It was reported that he was surrounded by dolphins and, more surprisingly, that he was not sunburned at all. The U.S. Coast Guard spotted Elián González and the two other survivors of a vessel carrying fourteen passengers from Cuba and immediately transfered Elián to Joe DiMaggio Children's Hospital. The two other survivors were rescued after they swam to Key Biscayne, a few miles from downtown Miami.

The story of Elián started similarly to that of many others who have risked their lives crossing the Florida Straits. The fact that he was six years old kept the public eye open and tearful as his story was related. His mother, Elizabet Brotons Rodríguez, had risked her life and that of her son on a crossing organized by her boyfriend, Lázaro Munero. In the months to come much would be made about his mother's intent. The critical question, should the boy remain in the United States or rejoin his father in Cuba, was often couched in the emotions surrounding a mother's sacrifice for her child. If he was returned, her life would have been given in vain, many in and outside of the Cuban American community felt. But try as they might, those wishing Elián to stay in the United States could not erase one incontrovertible fact: Elián had a father and the father wanted his son back. Ultimately, on Easter Saturday six months later, the father got his wish, but not before his son had played the role of protagonist in one of the most defining moments of the Cuban American experience in the United Sates.

Technically, Elián and the survivors of the tragic journey should have been returned to Cuba immediately. U.S. immigration policy under the Cuban Adjustment Act was amended in 1996 to include what is commonly referred to as a "wet feet, dry feet" policy. Cubans fleeing

The "wet feet, dry feet" policy in action. Law enforcement officials attempt to keep a Cuban rafter from reaching shore in South Florida, while bathers and the press look on. The man reached the beach and was therefore eligible for admission to the United States under a post-1996 U.S. policy that modified the implementation of the 1966 Cuban Refugee Adjustment Act. Had he been intercepted offshore, he would have been subject to deportation.

(The Miami Herald/Nuri Vallbona)

the island, if intercepted at sea, are unceremoniously returned to Cuba. If they manage to make it on land (dry feet), they are allowed to be reviewed for admittance, a pro forma procedure that guarantees a green card and permanent resident status. Elián had wet feet but was brought in for medical attention. The other survivors technically made it to land by being rescued after swimming to shore. In any case, they got lost in the shuffle and were allowed to stay.

Within two days, Elián was discovered to have relatives in Miami—distant relatives but relatives nevertheless. Lázaro González was his great-uncle, the uncle of Elián's father. Lázaro had arrived in the United States over a decade earlier and Elián had never met him or any other of his distant relatives in Miami. They were strangers to him. Nevertheless, on November 26th, Lazaro took Elián "home" to Little Havana.

In Cuba, Elián's father declared two days after the boy was found that he wanted his son back. Under normal circumstances, a father's wishes are the last words on such matters. There is nothing normal about dealing with Cuba or Cuban Americans, however. Temporary custody of the child had been granted to Lázaro and his family, who were becoming known as the "Miami family." To reverse that decision, the INS felt compelled to research the suitability of Juan Miguel as a parent. Implied in this research was the Cuban American allegation that in reality, since Juan Miguel González had waited two days to claim his son, he wished his son to stay in the United States and only the heavy hand of Fidel Castro had made him demand his return publicly.

The INS made two visits to the island to interview Juan Miguel. After the visits, the INS agreed that Juan Miguel was sincere in his wishes to have his boy returned. On January 6, 2000, then Attorney-General Janet Reno issued the decision: "This little boy, who has been through so much, belongs with his father" (Chardy, Nieves, and Viglucci 2000). This decision unleashed a series of events that have left an imprint on community relations throughout the Greater Miami area and on the image of Cubans in the United States.

Immediately after the decision, the Cuban American community declared that it would unleash massive protests. "Let's take action immediately with the objective of paralyzing Miami and paralyzing the airport," Alberto Hernández, a director of the Cuban American National Foundation urged other exile leaders at a meeting held following the announcement (Chardy, Nieves, and Viglucci 2000). On January 6, hundreds of Cuban Americans blocked intersections throughout the urban center and cut off access to the Port of Miami and Miami International Airport, protesting the decision.

If this tactic was designed to garner support for the Cuban American position, it failed. A large percentage of the wider Miami community felt put out by the traffic jams and public disturbances. The actions provided one of the many points of divisions between the Cubans and others in Miami.

For its part, the exile leadership was loath to hand over the boy to his father because it would constitute a propaganda victory for Fidel Castro. Jorge Mas Santos, the Chairman of the Cuban American National Foundation, succinctly voiced this opinion by stating, "This boy cannot become a trophy for Fidel" (Chardy, Nieves, and Viglucci 2000). This hard-line stance forced the U.S. Justice Department to establish and lift several return deadlines and engaged Janet Reno in unprecedented negotiations with the representatives of the "Miami family" on how to carry out the INS decision. Until the very end, the Miami negotiators were hoping for a miracle that would allow Elián to stay.

The "political correctness" within the Cuban American community of demanding that Elián stay in the United States was transmitted throughout the world in the words of Miami-Dade County Mayor

Alex Penelas. At a press conference on March 29, both Penelas and City of Miami Mayor Carollo claimed that their local police departments would not assist in aiding federal agents if they came to Miami to remove Elián, although Penelas subsequently clarified that police would keep the peace. If violence broke out, he warned the Clinton administration, "We hold you responsible" (Finefrock 2000).

This event, perhaps more than any other up to that time, served to polarize and concretize attitudes about the Cuban American community locally, nationally, and internationally. The Mayor's comments were particularly alienating to the non-Cuban communities of Greater Miami. At an ABC News Nightline town meeting on the campus of Florida International University, a non-Cuban white speaker from the audience chastised Mayor Penelas for his comments, reminding him that "he was elected to represent all of the citizens of Dade County."

Middle America concurred—as did Right America and Left America. The Miami Cubans were chastised across the board as ungrateful, unforgiving, and unpatriotic. "Why are they waving Cuban flags?" said an academic colleague from New York. "If they are so adamant that he stay here, since this place is so much better, why not wave American flags?"

As the Elián affair began to unravel, the various Miami communities did as well. Massive demonstrations were held supporting the claims of the Miami family. Across town, counter-demonstrations took place supporting the U.S. government's position and taking the opportunity to slam the Cuban American population. These counter-demonstrations brought together a motley crew. Good-ol' boys waving confederate flags and proudly holding signs exorting authorities to "Send them ALL back" stood next to African American families reminding Mayor Penelas that "You represent us too, Mayor."

Ultimately, the issue was resolved by the use of force. The INS forcibly entered the home of the Miami relatives before dawn on April 22. Fortunately, the small number of observers on the scene presented only token resistance to the well armed strike force. Pictures of the raid circumnavigated the globe via internet, television, and newspapers. Elián was reunited with his father a few hours later.

The Cuban American community vilified the government. A Cuban American professional in his late twenties exclaimed, "It's a betrayal. They betrayed us. We've been the most loyal supporters of the United States. How could they do this?" A sobbing woman, who has lived in Miami for thirty-eight years since coming from Cuba, proclaimed, "I thought it was the most unbelievable thing that I've seen in my life in the United States done to a poor family with a poor house." Cuban American pop stars Gloria Estefan and Andy García expressed their support for Elián remaining in the United States.

Street demonstration against Elián's return to Cuba, featuring U.S. and Cuban flags. Such demonstrations were a daily occurrence outside the home of the child's Miami relatives.

(The Miami Herald/Roberto Koltun)

Even moderate, broad-based organizations like the Cuban American National Council, criticized the federal government's strong arm tactics in a public statement: "We know no precedent for such an extraordinary operation, and cannot understand why the Justice Department deployed a commando tactical force, armed with semiautomatic weapons, face masks and tear gas that broke into the home of an innocent American family, the same family that the Justice Department itself had previously entrusted with Elián's care." Cuban American leaders of twenty-one exile organizations called for a citywide strike for the Tuesday following April 22 to "send a message of pain to the federal government and the nation about Elián's seizure." They sought to turn Miami into a "dead city" (Chardy 2000a, A1).

Throughout the Latino sections of Miami, the strike had a dramatic effect. In the heart of Little Havana, along Calle Ocho, nearly all businesses were closed as they were in Hialeah, the most thoroughly Latino municipality. Crowds gathered on the sidewalks and long convoys of vehicles slowed traffic, especially at key intersections. Vitriolic anti-government placards condemned the raid, calling President Clinton a communist and Reno a lesbian. Cuban flags were everywhere and many also displayed the U.S. flag, but they flew it upside down.

"We are staying away from work as a way to express our outrage, not only over Elián but also against what we see as a major change in U.S. policy—one that indicates an improvement in relations with Fidel Castro," declared a retired paint store owner who was one of the few pedestrians on Calle Ocho (Eighth St.), the main street of Little Havana. A Cuban American pediatrician closed his practice for the day. One of his sick patients visited a non-Cuban pediatrician for treatment. The non-Cuban pediatrician called the Cuban American pediatrician for information on the case. The Cuban American pediatrician took advantage of the call to assail the non-Cuban pediatrician for nearly an hour for working that day, passionately declaiming that no one did or could understand the hurt and pain of exiled Cubans (Chardy 2000b, A1).

About one-third of the students in public schools stayed home in a district that is over 50 percent Latino. At Florida International University, the local campus of the state university system which has a student body that is more than 50 percent Latino, about 700 administrative and support workers participated in the stoppage—including President Modesto Maidique, a Cuban American.

At least a few businesses closed out of fear after receiving threats of bombs or boycotts. Two Hialeah businesses—Denny's and Kmart—received bomb threats for staying open. Denny's closed after the second threat. Kmart remained open, but had police sweep the store. A Winn-Dixie grocery store in a mixed, but primarily Latino, neighborhood was evacuated after receiving a bomb threat. Even one church had to close because of threats. St. Kieran's Catholic Church, a mostly Latino congregation in Coconut Grove, closed after the church secretary received an anonymous call saying there would be a bomb if the church stayed open.

Before the raid, City Police Chief William O'Brien did not forewarn Mayor Carollo. After the raid, an angry Carollo publically stated that the Police Chief should be fired. The Mayor's hand-picked City Manager, Donald Warshaw—the only one with authority to fire the chief—refused. Carollo then fired the City Manager and the following day the Police Chief resigned. Both were replaced by Cuban Americans.

Non-Cubans were more forgiving of the government's tactics. Some were critical but insisted that the Miami family had forced the government's actions by refusing to hand over custody of the boy to the father. Some in other immigrant communities took the opportunity to highlight that the INS behaves similarly in hundreds of immigration cases a year, but that no one takes a second look until the victims are Cubans. The impact of the Elián case on Miami will persist for the foreseeable future. Given the disagreements between the city's ethnic communities over the issue, it is worthwhile highlighting one point of agreement among Cuban Americans, non-Cubans in Miami and national on-lookers: over 80 percent of each of these populations agreed that the events surrounding the Elián González affair hurt the interests of the Cuban American community.

IDENTITY AND THE LEGACY OF EXILE

The Elián case has given credence to the widely-held belief that Cuban-Americans, at least in Miami, are indeed a one-issue ethnic group and are monolithic in their views towards Cuba. No matter how much those Cubans with more moderate views try to distance themselves from the behavior of the Cuban community in Miami, the massive and broad show of support for the Miami family has had a compelling effect on local and national views towards Cuban Americans.

Despite the signs of diversity highlighted in previous chapters, the fact remains that during the Elián affair Cubans in the United States behaved as monolithically as they have ever done. A poll by the Miami Herald during the height of the controversy claimed that 90 percent of Cuban Americans in Miami-Dade County wanted Elián to stay. Even six months later, FIU reported in its Cuba Poll that, in thinking back to those days, 78 percent of Cuban American respondents in Miami held the opinion that Elián should stay. These are overwhelming numbers. They make arguments against a monolithic community rather abstract and unrelated to real community behavior.

What is also significant is the apparent schism among communities on the issue. Non-Cubans in Miami were significantly less likely to support Elián's stay (34 percent). Cuban Americans found even less support at the national level, where only 28 percent of non-Cubans supported keeping Elián with his "Miami family."

These figures clearly indicate a strong difference of opinion within the Miami-Dade population and give rise to two questions: Why did the Cuban American community respond as it did to the Elián González affair? and What impact will this reaction have on relations between Cubans and other ethnic groups in the community? The two questions are linked in that the reasons for the Cuban American response is closely tied to the persistence of a strong "exile identity" even as Cuba recedes as an issue of constant concern for the long-time residents and for the second generation. Elián González served to spark the exile identity of the Cuban American community, an opportunity that was exploited by important exile organizations. The most important is the Cuban American National Foundation (CANF), the organizational standard bearer of the "exile ideology," which used the Elián case to bolster its sagging community influence. Within hours of the boy's rescue from Florida waters, the CANF converted Elián, literally, into a poster child, distributing thousands of leaflets at the World Trade Organization meeting in Seattle with a picture of Elián beneath the headline: "Another child victim of Fidel Castro." After polls indicated that both young and old Cubans and other Latinos in Miami overwhelmingly believed that Elián should remain with his Miami relatives rather than return to Cuba to live with his father, CANF aggressively sought to incorporate younger Cubans into an organization that had primarily appealed to older exiles. It appointed a new, younger executive director, a thirty-five-year-old American-born Cuban, Joe García. García became the first CANF executive director born outside of Cuba. He promised a re-invigorated foundation with more sophisticated media efforts to educate the American people about Cuba (De Valle 2000 #3941). The CANF also appointed a non-Cuban former State Department expert on Cuba to head its Washington office and committed to organizational expansion that included purchasing a new building on Washington's Capitol Hill, refurbishing a historic landmark in Miami where Cuban refugees were processed in the 1960s, and doubling both its staff and annual budget. Not neglecting its traditional political role, CANF also singled out districts of Congressional adversaries for television advertisements and pledged to spend "whatever it takes" to protect the unyielding American policy it helped to create (Marquis 2000).

All of these efforts undoubtedly increased solidarity among Miami Cubans, and among Cubans in the rest of the United States. Twenty-nine-year-old Cristina Portuondo, for example, grew up in a small Virginia town, spoke with a Southern twang, and had little visible connection to Miami's exile community. But after Elián had been reunited with his father and taken to Washington, D.C., she ended up demonstrating in front of the Washington, D.C. area home of Cuba's top diplomat in the United States. "Here I am, the Cuban from Virginia and I'm one of the main ones that's been organizing," said Portuondo, who writes computer manuals for a living. "I've declared myself" (Robles 2000).

A large part of the credit, or blame, for the response of the Cuban community has to go to those keepers of the exile flame who were able to define Elián's situation not as one dealing primarily with family reunification but as one offering an opportunity for a political confrontation with Castro himself. They were able to define the situation this way by deftly connecting the ever present drone of exile politics with the strong emotional undercurrents of both exile and immigrant reality. It did not take much to unify a newcomer community with the stability of the Cuban Americans in Miami around the issue of a six-year-old's quality of life. Of course, Elián's life would be better here than in Cuba, most agreed, because a vast majority of Cubans are certain that their lives are better here than they would have been in Cuba, regardless of their reasons for leaving. As a Cuban American moderate said to Grenier, "He would have a much happier life here, really. Life in Cuba is tough and is not going to improve in our lifetime." The person who made this comment is a businesswoman who thinks little about the intricacies of exile politics.

This brings up a curious paradox: the exile ideology was so effective in imposing a monolithic definition of the Elián case on Cuban Americans precisely because of the diversity of the community. One characteristic of this diversity is that only a small percentage of the population is actively involved in exile politics. According to the FIU Cuba Poll 2000, less than three percent of Miami Cuban Americans report being active in organizations dealing directly with Cuba or Cuban issues, while 14 percent belong to other types of civic organizations. Cuba, for the most of the community on a daily basis, is a distant concern, yet it is the dominant current in the cultural waters of the Cuban American community in Miami. Because of this, many tend to respond in a knee-jerk fashion when the issue comes up. In the Elián case, no alternative voice was loud enough to elicit support. The approximately 22 percent (according to the FIU poll) of Miami Cuban Americans who felt that Elián should return were not heard and, in fact, many were fearful of expressing that opinion. "At work, I keep my mouth shut," said a Cuban American office worker to Grenier, "After this is all over I still have to work there and I don't think these people will forget [my opinion]." There simply was not a voice bold and loud enough to define the situation as one dealing with family reunification rather than as a blow against Castro. The child was a trophy for Fidel, not a son to Juan Miguel.

A WEDGE BETWEEN COMMUNITIES

Elián polarized Miami, with Latinos, primarily Cubans, advocating his remaining in Miami, and non-Latinos (along with a few Latinos) arguing that he should be reunited with his father in Cuba. Passions permeated relations, even with total strangers. María Hernández, a Colombian married to a Cuban, was driving to work when a pickup truck flying American flags pulled up beside her at a stoplight. The pickup truck driver, thinking she was a Cuban, rolled down a window and made an obscene gesture (Bragg 2000b).

The driver's gesture may have been extreme, but his opinion was typical. Various local polls showed both White and Black "Americans" felt strongly that the boy belonged with his father. Indeed, the pollster who conducted one of the studies, Rob Schroth, claimed, "In twenty years of studying polls in Dade, I have never seen results that set Cubans and the other two groups so far apart on an issue. The contrast is the starkest I've ever seen. It is truly a tale of two cities." About 90 percent of Blacks and 80 percent of Whites disapproved of County Mayor Penelas' threats to deny federal agents help from county police in repatriating Elián, as well as his attempt to blame any resulting violence on Reno and President Clinton. At least three-quarters of Miami's Cuban Americans, however, approved of both statements as well as Penelas' overall performance (Viglucci and Marrero 2000). Garth Reeves, the former publisher of Miami's Black newspaper, *The Miami Times*, claimed, "The Cuban exiles have shown such arrogance. They're saying, 'This is our town now, and, damn it, we run it. We make the decisions' to the exclusion of everyone else." Reeves asserted that Cuban Americans are a pampered minority that became a pampered majority, and now—at the first major setback for them in recent history—they denigrate the country that gave them a haven (Bragg 2000a).

These non-Latinos' reactions, however, were not primordial anti-immigrant feelings that had been simply waiting for the right moment to emerge. While some, perhaps even many, non-Latinos do harbor anti-Cuban sentiments, the case of Elián revealed that the form, expression, and perhaps even existence of these feelings emerges out of interactions between Cubans and non-Cubans. For years, Ann-Sofi Truby and a Cuban American who does maintenance at her house in South Miami had talked, "about our families, different things," said Ms. Truby, who has lived here nearly thirty years. They stopped talking, however, during the Elián situation. "I would stay inside while he was here," Ms. Truby said, because talk would end in argument. Ms. Truby, who is in her 60s and a non-Hispanic white, was one of the thousands who bought an American flag. She waved it from her Volvo whenever she saw people demonstrating for Elián to remain in the United States (Bragg 2000b). In a parallel fashion, many younger Miami Cubans who had never seriously considered their ethnic identity before, who had believed that they were "Americans" because they were different from their parents and grandparents, suddenly discovered that as the "real Americans" condemned them, they, too, could emotionally feel Cuban.

The Miami Herald also found itself internally riven by the Elián affair. Liz Balmaseda, a Cuban American Pulitzer Prize-winning columnist, complained to both the *Herald*'s publisher and its editor about what she saw as the paper's unsympathetic coverage of Miami's Cuban community. Fabiola Santiago, a senior writer at the Herald, felt the paper did a poor job of explaining how Cuban children were oppressed in Castro's regime (McQueen 2000). When reporter Meg Laughlin wrote a detailed account of Elián's private school and the right-wing textbooks used there, she came under fire from Barbara Gutiérrez, the Cuban American reader representative for the *Herald*, who writes a weekly critique of the paper's coverage: "The tone sounded editorial," Gutierrez says. "I think the message got through. There are certain ways of reporting a story where a community might feel it's inflammatory." A front-page editorial, ordered by publisher Alberto Ibarguen after the raid, declared: "The scenes of overwhelming force from yesterday at dawn shock the conscience.... The evidence clearly suggests that the Miami relatives were at last prepared to voluntarily deliver Elián to his father within a very short time." The *Herald's* own reporting, however, in the following days would undermine this contention.

Indeed, closer examination reveals the difficulty, perhaps even impossibility, of attaining "objectivity" on such an emotional issue. As the Herald's Gutierrez points out, "In this highly emotional story, what sounds straightforward to one group of readers sounds like pandering to another...each side wants the newspaper to report the news from their perspective." Position and passion are even inscribed in simple descriptive vocabulary. Roberto Vizcon, the news director of a Spanish-language television station said, "We would never broadcast that the boy is threatened with going back home. We would say, the boy is threatened with going back to Cuba...And, we would never call Fidel Castro president." To Miami Cubans, Castro must be referred to as a dictator (McQueen 2000).

The issue of media objectivity was also a point of contention among Miami's ethnic communities. The Cuba Poll showed that 62 percent of Miami Cuban Americans felt that the local media had behaved professionally and objectively in reporting the Elián story, but 60 percent accused the national media of being biased. Non-Cubans in Miami felt differently. Approximately 62 percent felt that the local media had behaved less than professionally in its coverage while 65 percent approved of the national media coverage.

Quite apart from questions of media objectivity, the Elián affair generated a tremendous backlash from local non-Latinos. City Hall was pelted with bananas, picking up on a local university professor's reference a couple of years before to Miami's "banana republic" government. County Mayor Penelas received numerous email messages blasting his statements that he would not assist federal officials in their efforts to reunite Elián with his father. A letter to the editor in the *Miami New Times* presented the view of many: "My husband and I have been residents of Dade County for over forty years and we have

Elián González clowns before the media in the front yard of the home of his Miami relatives. The objectivity of media coverage became an issue during the child's stay in the United States.

(The Miami Herald/C. M. Guerrero)

never been as angry or embarrassed at a speech by a Dade County mayor as the absurd speech you made yesterday. You are mayor of Cubans and Latins only, and the other residents of Dade County have no mayor. I can assure you that if there is a recall movement for you, we will sign it immediately. We will also do whatever we can to ensure you are not elected to office again. We are totally appalled, angry, and humiliated by this situation" (Miami New Times 2000). Arthur Teele, Jr., the City of Miami's only Black commissioner, claimed, "A number of people here are concerned and outraged because they believe the city of Miami has lost its balance and equilibrium." He added that Mayor Carollo's city government seemed anxious to exclude all but Cuban Americans precisely when interethnic tensions were running high (Bragg 2000a).

David Abraham, a professor at the University of Miami, explained, "This became a bizarre experience where family, flag, and police—all parts of the Republican trinity—were attacked by Cuban Americans. There was the firing of the police chief because he kept public order, and the desecration of the flag, and it was very disconcerting to middle Americans" (Bragg 2000a).

The Elián affair had similar negative national repercussions for Miami's Cuban community. Suddenly, the rest of America, which had previously cared little about Cuba, was paying attention to Cuba and Miami's Cubans. Representative Jim McDermott, Democrat of Washington, maintained that Miami's Cubans, "showed what they were really all about. They were ready to sacrifice one of their own kids, and they didn't really care about separating him from his father." For the first time since Fidel Castro assumed power forty years earlier, the U.S. Congress seriously considered easing the embargo on Cuba.

Both Cuban American and non-Cuban American leaders in Miami expressed concern that the Elián issue was both tearing apart the community and giving Miami a bad image. White "American" County manager Merritt Steirheim claimed, "Nobody in this town was without trauma: Cuban American, Haitian, Anglo, African American—everybody had anger, remorse, pain. My hope is that it was cathartic. The residue from Elián will be important for many, many years. We have a lot of wounds to heal." A few prominent Miami Cuban leaders even began to condemn fellow Miami Cubans, claiming that their focus on Elián and Castro's Cuba was myopic, and was hurting the Miami community. Some Miami Cuban leaders sought to ease tensions at the same time as they sought to explain to non-Cubans why they felt so strongly that Elián should remain in the United States. Reflecting the convergence of Latino and White "American" business elites, representatives from Mesa Redonda, an organization of Latino business and civic leaders, privately met with the City of Miami's mayor, Joe Carollo, and asked him to tone down his rhetoric, to try to build bridges to the rest of Miami's community. Mesa Redonda then had a joint meeting with the "Non-Group," the most important non-Hispanic white organization, and Broulé, a Black leadership fraternity. They jointly resolved to work toward unifying the community.

In Florida politics, the events surrounding the Elián affair have had a direct impact on at least two significant races. In 2001 Janet Reno announced her intentions to challenge Jeb Bush for governorship of the state in 2002. This reopened the old wounds and has given new life to old rhetoric. Many leaders in the Cuban American community expressed outrage at Reno's candidacy. While it is unlikely that Cuban Americans in Florida would cross party lines to vote for a Democrat, Janet Reno, as a local daughter made good, might have had a decent chance at pulling the Cuban vote had it not been for the role she played in the Elián affair. By all indications, she will be haunted by the Elián controversy up to the election day, 2002. All signs indicate that the measure of disdain captured in the FIU Cuba Poll 2000 six months after Elián returned home has not diminished.

The Elián affair also influenced the 2001 race for Mayor of Miami, in which Manny Diaz eventually defeated Maurice Ferre in a run off. Mr. Diaz had risen from obscurity to local prominence as a lawyer who represented Elián's Miami family in the attempt to keep the boy in the United States. Overzealous Ferre supporters allegedly doctored and distributed flyers with Diaz and Elián asking "Did he use and betray Elián to advance his own political career?" Diaz supporters, for their part, supposedly circulated rumors on Spanish-language radio stations that Ferre was supporting the Reno campaign. The lasting divisions created by the Elián affair were made painfully clear during a Ferre campaign visit to Temple Baptist Church. In endorsing Ferre, Rev. Richard Barry stated, "Elián makes the difference in this election. I heard it on the radio. A vote for Ferre is a vote for Janet Reno. I think Janet Reno is a good woman." The African American congregation burst into applause as Ferre cringed (Bridges and Corral 2001).

CONCLUSION

The Elián affair brought together many issues that characterize the Cuban American community in Miami and in the United States as a whole. It made clear that the exile legacy is very much alive, or at least capable of being revived, even if demographics and time conspire to make Cuba an increasingly distant reality. It also demonstrated how Cuban Americans inject homeland concerns into local politics and social dynamics, sometimes to their own detriment, yet always with a sense of solidarity and uniqueness which it claims others will never understand.

From the beginning of the Elián saga, the predominant voices among Cuban Americans defined the situation as a battle with Fidel Castro over a trophy, a trophy they were determined not to lose. The words "Not this time, Fidel" were heard frequently among those gathered outside the home of Elián's Miami relatives. During forty years, Fidel Castro may have triumphed over the exiles by retaining power in Cuba, but he was not, the exiles vowed, going to win this battle. The child was in their hands, in "their" city, a city where they had triumphed, a city they "controlled." They had homefield advantage on this one, and the trophy would be theirs. Even at the federal level, there was reason to be confident: the U.S. government had always proved willing to accommodate the exiles' agenda of combating Fidel Castro.

But for virtually everyone else in this country, Elián's case had nothing to do with doing battle with Fidel Castro. It had to do with returning a child to his father, an issue that deeply resonated with American values. It was a sorely misguided battle that was doomed from the start.

And so Fidel Castro won the trophy and yet another battle. The Cuban exile community felt, once again, defeated and betrayed, and even the parallel with the Bay of Pigs fiasco was noted. Perhaps this loss will eventually force a cold reexamination of the exile strategy, or at least an acknowledgment that the battle for Elián had been a misstep. After all, and as stated earlier, 82 percent of Cubans in Miami interviewed by the FIU Cuba Poll agreed that the interests of the Cuban American community were hurt by the events surrounding the case of Elián.

But part of the legacy of exile legacy is its irrational character, based as it is on emotion and passion. The FIU Cuba poll, taken six months after the child was returned to Cuba, also asked Cubans in Miami: "From the beginning of the Elián situation to now, have you had the same opinion on what should have been done, or were there changes over time in what you thought should be done?" Those who answered that they held the same opinion: 93.5 percent.

9

Conclusion

Exiles Much Longer?

I came to this country when Christmas festivities were about to begin. I remember my first day working at a factory. A Cuban co-worker, realizing that I had just arrived from the island, said with sincere enthusiasm: "Boy, are you lucky. This is the first and the last lechoncito *(little pig) that you are going to eat in exile. The next one will be in a free Cuba." The man was referring to our custom of celebrating* Nochebuena, Christmas *eve, by roasting a pig. This year, we will roast* lechoncito *No. 33.*

José A. Vargas, Miami
Letters to the Editor
The Miami Herald
December 10, 2001, p. 6B

Mr. Vargas' letter poignantly encapsulates what has been the theme of this book: the legacy of exile. After thirty-three years in this country, he has not forgotten that his departure from the island was only temporary. He is still counting the pigs that should have been eaten in the island where he was born. This exile ethos of the homeland waiting to be reclaimed runs like a leitmotif through the history of the Cuban presence in the United States, starting with Father Félix Varela, who came in 1823. For Mr. Vargas, there are *lechoncitos* waiting to be eaten at *Nochebuenas* in a reclaimed "free Cuba." For José Martí it was all about the majestic royal palms that dot the Cuban countryside. "The palms," he wrote from New York, "are like waiting brides."

An identity as exiles has colored all aspects of the life of Cubans in the United States. It has resulted in an inordinate allocation of resources, including emotional energy, towards the primary task of reclaiming the homeland; it has shaped the social life of the Cuban American community and the focus of its voluntary associations; it has reinforced a sense of exceptionalism, setting themselves apart from other immigrant and Latino groups; it has made the relationship with the government of the homeland a perennially conflictive one; it has determined the nature of their participation in the political life of the new country. In short, the condition of exile has defined the purpose of the community and its reason for being here, and it is the condition that has largely shaped the image most Americans have of them.

The contradiction is that this exile ethos has not kept Cubans from attaining success as immigrants. They have achieved both economic and political success within the first generation, a dramatic exception to most immigrant communities' experiences, and they have contributed significantly to the transformation of Miami into the capital of the Caribbean.

If indeed exile has defined the condition of Cubans in the United States, then the biggest issue as we look toward the future is what will happen when they are no longer exiles. That is, what will this group look like when the entire context that has shaped their very identity changes dramatically?

There is a combination of ways in which the context of the exile condition may change. One is through a generational transition as new generations, born in the United States, come of age. The other is through a fundamental change in the relationship with the homeland. We have argued throughout this book that the predominant force in the creation of the world of Cuban Americans is the early wave of exiles, the displaced elites and others marked by the political confrontation of the early 1960s. They have been the keepers of the flame of the anti-Castro struggle. They established the bases for the creation of the enclave, but that was nearly forty years ago. Will they not soon be replaced by other generations and other waves of arrivals whose commitment to the exile agenda is more tenuous?

Figure 9.1 presents the changes since the 1970 U.S. Census in the various components, by wave of arrival and nativity, of the Cuban-origin population of the United States. The figure shows a significant erosion through time in the proportional representation of the early exiles. In 1970, those arriving between 1960 and 1964 represented slightly more than thirty percent. If we add those arriving during the Airlift, the proportion exceeded two-thirds of the Cuban-origin population in 1970.

By the end of the twentieth century, however, the growth of the U.S.-born and the arrival of new waves had combined with mortality to whittle down the proportion of early exiles. Those arriving from 1960 to 1964 and during the Airlift barely accounted for a third of all Cubans in the United States in 1997.

Another way of looking at Figure 9.1, however, is to see, surprisingly, that the picture has not changed even more in three decades. Given the time that has elapsed, for example, the relative growth of the U.S.-born is fairly sluggish, reflecting the low fertility discussed

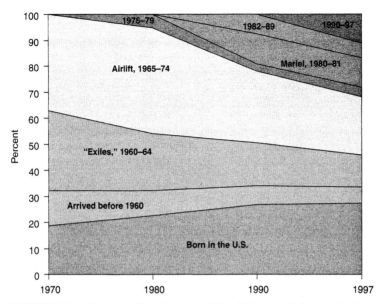

FIGURE 9.1   Percent distribution of the Cuban-origin population of the U.S., by nativity and year of arrival of the Cuban-born, 1970–1997

Source: Compiled and drawn by the authors from data in the decennial U.S. censuses and the Current Population reports, U.S. Bureau of the Census.

in Chapter 5. The Airlift arrivals declined drastically, no doubt because of the high proportion of the elderly among them, as also noted in Chapter 5.

But the early exiles, 1960–1964, show, as a group, a great deal more survivability. This is also not surprising, since we noted that this wave included a large number of families with children. The latter can be expected to survive well into the twenty-first century. The early exiles are therefore not a group that, in demographic terms, will be gone anytime soon.

Demographics aside, the influence of the early exiles is also likely to linger. They have firmly planted the banner of the exile ideology as the predominant perspective for looking at the homeland. The Elián González saga showed just how much the anti-Castro cause was capable of mobilizing groups other than the early exiles within the community. The anti-Castro cause has been the core of the political culture of Cuban Americans. No doubt newer generations and arrivals do not, overall, have the same level of commitment to that cause, nor is the homeland so central to their agenda. Change has already been occurring, as noted in Chapter 7, in the predominance of the exile ideology. But it would be a mistake to prematurely announce its demise as a simple function of a demographic transition.

Of course, one way things will change much more dramatically is if there is a transformation in the relationship with the homeland. That could happen with the death of Fidel Castro, for in that case the "personalized" conflict would be over, especially if Cuba undergoes a significant transformation as a result. The exile ideology has a strong oppositional nature. It would not be sustainable without its nemesis.

The relationship with the homeland would also change if—and when—relations between the United States and Cuba become normalized. Ending the isolation of Cuba would potentially permit a normal flow of people and goods between the two countries. There would be a boom in that flow, with Cuban Americans in the thick of it, given their interest in their homeland and the likelihood that Miami will be the axis of that expanded contact.

The passing of the exile generation, the death of Castro, the normalization of relations with Cuba, all these things will occur sometime in the future. They are impending crossroads in the history of Cubans in the United States, for they represent an end to the context of exile.

Will many Cuban Americans return to Cuba permanently once these conditions occur? The FIU Cuba Poll has consistently shown that only about 20 percent of Cubans interviewed in the United States said they would. We have been careful throughout the book to use the phrase "recovery of" the homeland and not "return to" to describe the exile ideology. The former is the abiding interest in seeing the homeland out of the hands of the Castro government. Returning is something else, especially if a large portion of the exile generation has already passed away in the United States. Mr. Vargas hopes to live to that *Nochebuena* when he can eat his *lechoncito* in Cuba, but he will probably not be living permanently there when he does so. Moving back permanently may be not be necessary to fulfill the exile dream of "recovering" Cuba. The distance between Havana and Miami is much closer than the distance from Miami to, say, Disney World in Orlando. The aerial jump across the Florida Straits takes all of twenty minutes. With 1.2 million persons of Cuban origin living in the United States, a majority of them in Miami, and with the opening of Cuba as a tourist destination for Americans, there will probably be an air shuttle system between Miami and Havana that will rival that between New York and Washington, D.C. Such a development would fundamentally transform Cuban Miami.

When they largely cease to be exiles, Cubans in the United States will no doubt start moving closer to other U.S. immigrant groups in terms of their political, social, and economic agenda. There will probably be a greater cultural and political integration with other Latino groups. There are already indications that the panethnic labels so vehemently rejected by the first generation have made inroads among Cuban Americans born in this country. The Children of Immigrants Longitudinal Study found that among the Cuban-origin children in senior high school in Miami, thirty percent identified as "Hispanic" or "Latino" (Pérez 2001, 107–108). An Hispanic or Latino identity is not derived from their parents. Virtually none of those children indicated that their Cuban-born parents identified as anything other than "Cuban."

But there probably will be limits to the degree of integration and identification with other immigrant and Latino groups. A strong insular identity and a sense of exceptionalism are firm tenets of Cuban culture, preceding, by centuries, the creation of the modern Cuban presence in the United States. The bumper sticker "I am not Hispanic, I am Cuban," is likely to be around Miami for a long time to come, perhaps on the car of Mr. Vargas' grandchild, who will no doubt celebrate *Nochebuena* with a *lechoncito*.

References

Aguirre, Benigno E.
1981   The Marital Stability of Cubans in the United States. *Ethnicity 8:* 387–405.

Associated Press
2001   Gore Won, Blacks Tell Poll. *Miami Herald,* 20 February, B9.

Baltar Rodríguez, José
1997   *Los chinos de Cuba: apuntes etnográficos.* La Habana: Fundación Fernando Ortiz.

Bernal, Guillermo
1982   Cuban Families. In Monica McGoldrick, John Pearce, and Joseph Giordano (eds.), *Ethnicity and Family Therapy* (pp. 187–207). New York: The Guilford Press.

Bettinger-López, Caroline
2000   *Cuban-Jewish Journeys: Searching for Identity, Home, and History in Miami.* Knoxville: University of Tennessee Press.

Bosch, Juan
1955   *Cuba, la isla fascinante.* Reprint. Santo Domingo: Editorial Alpha y Omega, 1987.

Boswell, Thomas D. and James R. Curtis
1984   *The Cuban-American Experience: Culture, Images and Perspectives.* Totowa, NJ: Rowman and Allenheld.

Bragg, Rick
2000a   Legacy of a Cuban boy: Miami City Hall is Remade. *New York Times,* 10 May, A20.
2000b   Fight over Cuban boy leaves scars in Miami. *New York Times,* 30 June, A12.

Branch-Brioso, Karen, Tim Henderson, and Alfonso Chardy
2000   The Real Power in Dade. *The Miami Herald,* 3 September, A1.

Bridges, T. and O. Corral
2001   Elián, Reno Fallout at Core of Race. *The Miami Herald,* 12 November, B1–2.

Castellanos, Gerardo
1935   *Motivos de Cayo Hueso.* La Habana: Ucar, García y Cía.

Castro, Max J.
1992   The Politics of Language in Miami. In Guillermo J. Grenier and Alex Stepick III (eds.), *Miami Now: Immigration, Ethnicity, and Social Change* (pp. 109–132).

Census National Board of Cuba
1920   *Census of the Republic of Cuba 1919.* La Habana: Maza, Arroyo, y Caso.

Chardy, Alfonso
2000a   Businesses Set for Shutdown. *The Miami Herald*, 2 April 25, A1, 5.
2000b   Parts of Dade Shut Down: Massive Protest Mostly Peaceful. *The Miami Herald*, 26 April, A1.

Chardy, Alfonso, Gail Epstein Nieves, and Andres Viglucci
2000   INS: Send Elián Back, Cuban Exiles Vow Widespread Protests. *The Miami Herald*, 6 January, A1.

Clark, Juan
1975   The Exodus from Revolutionary Cuba (1959–1974): A Sociological Analysis. Ph.D. dissertation, University of Florida.

De Valle, Elaine
2000   CANF Adds to its Leadership Ranks. *The Miami Herald*, 21 May, B1.

Dluhy, Milan J. and C. E. Krebs
1987   *Dade County, Florida: A needs assessment of the 60 and over population.* Miami: Southeast Florida Center on Aging, Florida International University.

Díaz-Briquets, Sergio
1983   *The Health Revolution in Cuba.* Austin: University of Texas Press.

Díaz-Briquets, Sergio and Lisandro Pérez
1981   Cuba: The Demography of Revolution. *Population Reference Bureau Bulletin Series 36:* 1–41.

Didion, Joan.
1987   *Miami.* New York: Simon and Schuster.

Dugger, Cynthia
1987   MMAP Losing Punch, Leaders Say. *The Miami Herald*, 17 July, C5.

Fagen, Richard R., Richard A. Brody, and Thomas J. O'Leary
1968   *Cubans in Exile: Disaffection and the Revolution.* Stanford, CA: Stanford University Press.

Feldstein Soto, Luis
1990   Carey Ousted from Metro: Teele, Winn elected. Valdes Faces Runoff. *The Miami Herald*, 5 September, A1.

Fernandez-Kelly, Patricia and Ana Garcia
1989   Informalization at the Core: Hispanic Women, Home Work and the Advanced Capitalist State. In Alejandro Portes, Manuel Castell, and Lauren Benton (eds.), *The Informal Economy: Studies in Advanced and Less Developed Countries* (pp. 247–264). Baltimore: The Johns Hopkins University Press.

Ferree, Myra Marx
1979   Employment Without Liberation: Cuban Women in the United States. *Social Science Quarterly 60:* 35–50.

Finefrock, Don
2000   Penelas' Hot Talk Assessed as Error. *The Miami Herald*, 9, April, B1.

Fitzpatrick, Joseph P. and Douglas T. Gurak
1979   *Hispanic Intermarriage in New York City.* New York: Fordham University Hispanic Research Center.

García, María Cristina
1996   *Havana USA: Cuban Exiles and Cuban Americans in South Florida, 1959–1994.* Berkeley: University of California Press.

Geldof, Lynn
1991   *Cubans: Voices of Change.* New York: St. Martin's Press.

Grenier, Guillermo J.
1992   The Cuban-American Labor Movement in Dade County: An Emerging
        Immigrant Working Class. In Guillermo J. Grenier and Alex Stepick III
        (eds.), *Miami Now: Immigration, Ethnicity, and Social Change*
        (pp. 133–159).

Grenier, Guillermo J. and Lisandro Pérez
1996   Miami Spice: The Ethnic Cauldron Simmers. In Silvia Pedraza and
        Rubén G. Rumbaut (eds.), *Origins and Destinies: Immigration, Race, and
        Ethnicity in America* (pp. 360–372). Belmont, CA: Wadsworth Publishing
        Company.
1998   Refugees to Immigrants: The Rise of the Cuban American Community
        in Miami. In Gregory R. Campbell (ed.), *Many Americas: Critical Perspec-
        tives on Race, Racism, and Ethnicity* (pp. 217–229). Dubuque, IA: Kendall/
        Hunt Publishing.

Grenier, Guillermo J. and Max Castro
1999   Triadic Politics: Ethnicity, Race and Politics in Miami, 1959–1998. *Pacific
        Historical Review* 68(2): 273–292.

Guanche, Jesús
1996   *Componentes étnicos de la nación cubana.* La Habana: Ediciones Unión.

Herman, M.
1995   *A Tale of Two Cities: Testing Explanations for Riot Violence in Miami, Florida
        and Los Angeles, California, 1980, 1992.* Washington, DC: American Socio-
        logical Association.

Hernández Travieso, Antonio
1984   *El Padre Varela: Biografía del forjador de la conciencia cubana.* 2nd ed.
        Miami: Ediciones Universal.

International Bank for Reconstruction and Development
1951   *Report on Cuba.* Washington, DC: International Bank for Reconstruction
        and Development.

Knight, Franklin W.
1970   *Slave Society in Cuba During the Nineteenth Century.* Madison: University
        of Wisconsin Press.

Kurtines, William M. and Luke Miranda
1980   Differences in Self and Family Role Perception among Acculturating
        Cuban-American College Students: Implications for the Etiology of
        Family Disruption among Migrant Groups. *International Journal of Inter-
        cultural Relations* 4: 167–184.

Lamphere, Louise, ed.
1992   *Structuring Diversity: Ethnographic Perspectives on the New Immigration.*
        Chicago: University of Chicago Press.

Lamphere, Louise, Alex Stepick, and Guillermo Grenier, eds.
1994   Newcomers in the Workplace: Immigrants and the Restructuring of the
        U.S. Economy. Philadelphia: Temple University Press.

Levine, Robert M.
1993   *Tropical Diaspora: The Jewish Experience in Cuba.* Gainesville: University
        Press of Florida.

Loescher, Gilbert and John Scanlan
  1986   *Calculated Kindness: Refugees and the Half-Open Door, 1945 to the Present.*
          New York: The Free Press.
Marquis, Christopher
  2000   Cuban American Lobby on the Defensive. *New York Times,* 30 June, A12.
Marrero, Leví
  1987   *Cuba en la década de 1950: Un país en desarrollo.* San Juan, Puerto Rico:
          Ediciones Capiro.
Masud-Piloto, Felix Roberto
  1988   With Open Arms: Cuban Migration to the United States. Totowa, NJ:
          Rowman & Littlefield.
  1996   From Welcomed Exiles to Illegal Immigrants. Lanham, MD: Rowman &
          Littlefield.
Maza Miquel, Manuel
  1990   *El alma del negocio y el negocio del alma, testimonios sobre la iglesia y la so-*
          ciedad en Cuba, 1878–1894. Santo Domingo: Pontificia Universidad
          Católica Madre y Maestra.
McCadden, Joseph and Helen M. McCadden
  1984   *Félix Varela: Torch Bearer from Cuba.* 2nd ed. San Juan, Puerto Rico:
          United States Catholic Historical Society.
McQueen, M.
  2000   In the Cauldron. *American Journalism Review,* 4 December.
Metro-Dade County
  1993   *A Minority-owned and Women-owned Business Discrimination Study: Exec-*
          utive Summary. Miami: Metro-Dade County.
  1994   *Black Elected Officials in Dade County.* Miami: Metro-Dade County.
Miami New Times
  2000   Letters to the Editor, 22 April.
Mills, C. Wright
  1959   *The Sociological Imagination.* New York: Oxford University Press.
Mohl, Raymond A.
  1990   On the Edge: Blacks and Hispanics in Metropolitan Miami Since 1959.
          The Florida Historical Quarterly, 37–56.
Moreno Fraginals, Manuel
  1978   *El ingenio, complejo económico social cubano del azúcar.* Revised edition, 3
          vols. La Habana: Editorial de Ciencias Sociales.
  1995   *Cuba/España, España/Cuba: Historia común.* Barcelona: Giraldo Monda-
          dori, S.A.
Mormino, Gary R. and George E. Pozzetta
  1987   *The Immigrant World of Ybor City: Italians and their Latin Neighbors in*
          Tampa, 1885–1985. Urbana: University of Illinois Press.
Ortiz, Fernando
  1940   *Contrapunteo cubano del tabaco y el azúcar.* Reprint. Santa Clara: Univer-
          sidad Central de Las Villas, 1963.
Pedraza, Silvia
  1996   Cuba's Refugees: Manifold Migrations. In Silvia Pedraza and Rubén G.
          Rumbaut (eds.), *Origins and Destinies: Immigration, Race, and Ethnicity in*
          America (pp. 263–279). Belmont, CA: Wadsworth Publishing
          Company.

Pedraza-Bailey, Silvia
  1985   *Political and Economic Migrants in America: Cubans and Mexicans.* Austin: University of Texas Press.
Pérez, Lisandro
  1986a   Cubans in the United States. *Annals of the American Academy of Political and Social Science 487* (September): 126–137.
  1986b   Immigrant Economic Adjustment and Family Organization: The Cuban Success Story Reexamined. *International Migration Review 20*(1): 4–20.
  1992   Cuban Miami. In Guillermo J. Grenier and Alex Stepick III (eds.), *Miami Now: Immigration, Ethnicity, and Social Change* (pp. 83–108). Gainesville: University Press of Florida.
  1994a   Cuban Catholics in the United States. In Jay P. Dolan and Jaime R. Vidal (eds.), *Puerto Rican and Cuban Catholics in the U.S., 1900–1965* (pp. 145–208). Notre Dame: University of Notre Dame Press.
  1994b   Cuban Families in the United States. In Ronald L. Taylor (ed.), *Minority Families in the United States: A Multicultural Perspective* (pp. 95–112). Englewood Cliffs, NJ: Prentice-Hall.
  1996   The Households of Children of Immigrants in South Florida: An Exploratory Study of Extended Family Arrangements. In Alejandro Portes (ed.), *The New Second Generation* (pp. 108–118). New York: Russell Sage Foundation.
  1999   The End of Exile? A New Era in U.S. Immigration Policy Toward Cuba. In Max J. Castro (ed.), *Free Markets, Open Societies, Closed Borders? Trends in International Migration and Immigration Policy in the Americas* (pp. 197–211). Coral Gables, FL: North-South Center Press at the University of Miami.
  2000   De Nueva York a Miami: El desarrollo demográfico de las comunidades cubanas en Estados Unidos. *Revista Encuentro de la Cultura Cubana* 15(Winter): 13–23.
  2001   Growing Up in Cuban Miami: Immigration, the Enclave, and New Generations. In Rubén G. Rumbaut and Alejandro Portes (eds.) *Ethnicities: Children of Immigrants in America* (pp. 91–125). Berkeley and New York: University of California Press and Russell Sage Foundation.
Pérez, Louis A. Jr.
  1988   *Cuba: Between Reform and Revolution.* New York: Oxford University Press.
  1999   *On Becoming Cuban: Identity, Nationality, and Culture.* Chapel Hill: The University of North Carolina Press.
Pérez Firmat, Gustavo
  1994   *Life on the Hyphen: The Cuban-American Way.* Austin: University of Texas Press.
Perez-Stable, Marifeli and Miren Uriarte
  1990   Latinos in a Changing U.S. Economy: Cuban-Americans in Miami. Unpublished paper, SUNY, Old Westbury.
Porter, Bruce and Marvin Dunn
  1984   *The Miami Riot of 1980: Crossing the Bounds.* Lanham, MD: Lexington Books.
Portes, Alejandro
  1969   Dilemmas of a Golden Exile: Integration of Cuban Refugee Families in Milwaukee. *American Sociological Review 34:* 505–518.
  1995   Children of Immigrants: Segmented Assimilation and its Determinants. In Alejandro Portes (ed.), *The Economic Sociology of Immigration: Essays*

on Networks, Ethnicity, and Entrepreneurship (pp. 248–280). New York: Russell Sage Foundation.

Portes, Alejandro and Robert L. Bach
1985   Latin Journey: Cuban and Mexican Immigrants in the United States. Berkeley: University of California Press.

Portes, Alejandro, Juan Clark, and Robert Manning
1985   After Mariel: A Survey of the Resettlement Experiences of 1980 Cuban Refugees in Miami. Cuban Studies, 15(2): 37–59.

Portes, Alejandro and Alex Stepick
1985   Unwelcome Immigrants: The Labor Market Experiences of 1980 (Mariel) Cuban and Haitian Refugees in South Florida. American Sociological Review 50(August): 493–514.

Portes, Alejandro and Alex Stepick
1993   City on the Edge: The Transformation of Miami. Berkeley: University of California Press.

Portuondo, Fernando
1975   Historia de Cuba, 1492–1898. 6th ed. La Habana: Editorial Nacional de Cuba, 1965. Reprint, La Habana: Instituto Cubano del Libro.

Poyo, Gerald E.
1989   With All, and for the Good of All: The Emergence of Popular Nationalism in the Cuban Communities of the United States, 1848–1898. Durham, NC: Duke University Press.

Prieto, Yolanda
1987   Cuban Women in the U.S. Labor Force: Perspectives on the Nature of Change. Cuban Studies 17: 73–91.

Queralt, Magaly
1983   The Elderly of Cuban Origin: Characteristics and Problems. In R. L. McNeely and J. N. Colen (eds.), Aging in Minority Groups (pp. 50–65). Beverly Hills: Sage Publications.

Ramirez, Deborah
2000   Upheaval to Upbeat. Sun-Sentinel, 23 April.

República de Cuba
1939   Gaceta Oficial 28: 2189–2193.
1950   Gaceta Oficial 48: 27553–27554.

Reveron, Derek
1989   Violence, Delays Hurt Renewal in Black Dade. The Miami Herald, 13 February 13, A-1.

Rich, Cynthia Jo
1974   Pondering the Future: Miami's Cubans after 15 Years. Race Relations Reporter, 5.

Rieff, David
1987   Going to Miami: Exiles, Tourists, and Refugees in the New America. Boston: Little, Brown and Company.

Rivas, Robert
1980   Sepultan en Cayo Hueso a toda la familia de Ibis Guerrero. El Miami Herald, 21 May.

Rivero Muñiz, José
1958   Los cubanos en Tampa. Revista Bimestre Cubana 74(January–June): 5–140.

Robles, Frances
2000   Elián Saga Awakens Activists to the Cause. *The Miami Herald*, 22 May, B1.

Rodríguez Chávez, Ernesto
1999   *Cuban Migration Today*. La Habana: Editorial José Martí.

Stack, John F. Jr. and Christopher L. Warren
1992   The Reform Tradition and Ethnic Politics: Metropolitan Miami Confronts the 1990s. In Guillermo J. Grenier and Alex Stepick III (eds.), *Miami Now: Immigration, Ethnicity, and Social Change* (pp. 160–185). Gainesville: University Press of Florida.

Steinback, Robert
2001   Ethnic Groups Talk in Post-Elián Year. *The Miami Herald*, 11 March, B1.

Stepick, Alex
1989   Miami's Two Informal Sectors. In Alejandro Portes, Manuel Castell, and Lauren Benton (eds.), *The Informal Economy: Studies in Advanced and Less Developed Countries* (pp. 111–131). Baltimore: The Johns Hopkins University Press.

Stepick, Alex
1990   Community Growth versus Simply Surviving: The Informal Sectors of Cubans and Haitians in Miami. In M. E. Smith (ed.), *Perspectives on the Informal Economy* (183–205). Washington, DC: University Press of America.

Stepick, Alex, Guillermo J. Grenier, Max Castro, and Marvin Dunn
        This Land is Our Land: Immigrants and Power in Miami. Berkeley: University of California Press, forthcoming.

Szapocznik, Jose, Mercedes A. Scopetta, and Wayne Tillman
1978   What Changes, What Remains the Same, and What Affects Acculturative Change in Cuban Immigrant Families. In Jose Szapocznik and Maria Cristina Herrera (eds.), *Cuban Americans: Acculturation, Adjustment and the Family* (pp. 35–49). Washington, DC: National Coalition of Hispanic Mental Health and Human Services Organization.

Szapocznik, Jose and Roberto Hernandez
1988   The Cuban American Family. In Charles H. Mindel, Robert W. Habenstein, and Roosevelt Wright, Jr. (eds.), *Ethnic Families in America* (3rd ed., 160–172). New York: Elsevier.

Thomas, Hugh
1971   *Cuba: The Pursuit of Freedom*. New York: Harper & Row.

Torres, Maria de los Angeles
1999   *In the Land of Mirrors: Cuban Exile Politics in the United States*. Ann Arbor: The University of Michigan Press.

Triay, Victor Andres
1998   *Fleeing Castro: Operation Pedro Pan and the Cuban Children's Program*. Gainesville: University of Florida Press.

U.S. National Archives and Records Service
1958   *Passenger Lists of Vessels Arriving in New York, 1820–1897*. Roll 422 (January 2–February 24, 1880). Washington, DC: U.S. National Archives and Records Service.

U.S. War Department
1900   *Report on the Census of Cuba 1899*. Washington, DC: U.S. Government Printing Office.

Viglucci, Andres
1999   Dade Poor Get Housing Boost. *The Miami Herald*, 28 February, B1.

Viglucci, Andres and D. Marrero
2000   Poll reveals widening split over Elián. *The Miami Herald*, 9 April 9, A1.

Viglucci Andres and W. Yardley
2001   South Florida: A Region in flux. Young Families, Latin Immigrants Making Area their Home. *The Miami Herald*, 23 May, A1.

Westfall, L. Glenn
1977   Don Vicente Martínez Ybor, the Man and his Empire: Development of the Clear Havana Industry in Cuba and Florida in the Nineteenth Century. Ph.D. diss., University of Florida.

Index

Aborigines, 29
Abraham, David, 112
Africa
  Cuban military presence in, 34
  importance in Cuban culture,
    37–39
  migration from, 38
African-Americans in Miami, 47,
    51, 74–83
  bilingualism and, 78, 81
  boycott by, 80
  businesses of, 74–75
  perceptions of Cubans, 77–79
  political strength of, 76–77
  relations with Cubans, 74–83
  riots by, 74
  settlement patterns of, 76
  visit by Mandela and, 79–80
Afro-Cuban cults, 39
Aging, 62–63
Aguilera, Francisco Vicente, 16
American Civil Liberties Union, 80
Arnaz, Desiderio (Desi) Jr., 20

Balmaseda, Liz, 110
Barry, Richard (Rev.), 114
Bay of Pigs, 33, 90, 115
Bilingual education, 54
Bilingualism, 78
Birth rate, 65–66
Black Lawyers' Association, 80
Botánicas, 39
Boycott Coalition, 80
Brotons Rodríguez, Elizabeth, 101
Broulé, 113

Camarioca, 23
Capital, types of, 51–52
  economic, 52
  political, 53–54
  social, 54–55
Carollo, Joe, 104, 106, 112, 113
Castro, Fidel
  Elián González case and, 103,
    108, 109, 111, 114–115
  government of, 1, 87, 95
  opposition to, 87, 89, 92, 93,
    119–120
Castro, Max, 3, 99
Catholic Church, 41–42, 58–59
Central Intelligence Agency
  (CIA), 53
Chicago, 2
Children, unaccompanied, 23
Children of Immigrants
  Longitudinal Study
  (CILS), 3, 62, 121
China
  importance in Cuban
    culture, 40
  migration from, 40
Cigar manufacturing, 18–20
Civil Rights Act, 46
Civil Rights movement, 1, 76
Clinton, William, 104, 106, 110
Colombians, 82
Comedores, 96
Congress (U.S.), 85, 91
Cuban Adjustment Act, 101–102
Cuban American National Council
  (CANC), 105

Cuban American National
    Foundation (CANF), 91, 98,
    103, 108
Cuban Democracy (Torricelli) Act,
    91
Cuban Liberty and Democratic
    Solidarity (Helms-Burton)
    Act, 91
Cuban migration to the U.S., 15–27
    after 1959, 20–25
    Airlift, 23–24, 58, 89, 119
    before 1959, 16–20
    conflict with U.S. and, 88
    demographic selectivity of, 59–60
    early exiles, 23, 58, 119
    family structure and, 58–60
    Mariel, 24–25, 89
    1994 and 1995 accords, 94–95
    Rafter Crisis, 25
    revolution in Cuba and, 22–23, 58
    socioeconomic selectivity of,
        58–59
Cuban Refugee Program, 53, 63, 89

Democratic Party, 89
Diaz, Manny, 114
Díaz-Balart, Lincoln, 98
Diversity
    cultural, 35–40
    political, 94–95
Divorce, 66–67

Economic adjustment, 48–51
Eisenhower, Dwight D., 90
Elderly, 51, 59–63, 89, 96
El Nuevo Herald, 2
El Portal, 81
Embargo, 92
Emotionalism, 92–93
Enclave
    characteristics of, 49–51
    development of, 46–51
    female employment and the, 64
    social networks and, 54–55
    social solidarity in the, 54, 87

English Only, 81
Entrepreneurship, 42, 49–50, 58, 68
Estefan, Gloria, 81, 104
Exceptionalism, 30–35, 117, 121

Family, 57–69
    Cuban laws related to, 59
    economic adjustment and, 67–68
    migration and structure of, 58–60
    organization of, 61–97
    vists of, to Cuba, 94
Fatalism, 42
Fernández Piérola y López de
    Luzuriaga, Ramón, 40–41
Ferre, Maurice, 114
Florida City, 81
Florida International University
    (FIU), 80, 104, 106
    Cuba Poll, 3, 88, 92, 93, 95, 107,
        109, 111, 113, 115, 120
Florida Legislature, 77, 98
Flota system, 31, 36
Ford Changing Relations Project, 3

García, Andy, 104
García, Joe, 108
Gender roles, 64, 66
González, Elián, 27, 92, 98,
    101–115, 119
    media objectivity and, 111
González, Juan Miguel, 102–103, 109
González, Lázaro, 102
Greater Miami Chamber of
    Commerce (GMCC), 71–73
Greater Miami Convention and
    Visitors Bureau, 80
Grenier, Guillermo J., 3, 5–8
Gutiérrez, Barbara, 111

Haitians, 79–80, 82
Hastings, Alcee, 81
Havana, 31–33, 40, 41–42, 120
    role in Spanish empire, 31–32
    secular character of, 41–42
Hernández, Alberto, 103

Hernández, Liván, 85–86
Hialeah, 96, 98, 105
Hialeah Gardens, 98
Hispanic Builders Association, 98
Homeland, primacy of, 87–89
Homestead, 85–86

Ibarguen, Alberto, 111
Identity, exile, 87, 107–108, 117–118
Ideology, exile, 86–93
  changes in, 93–95
  Elián González case and, 108–109
  fall of Berlin Wall and, 94
  pluralism in, 95
Immigration and Naturalization
  Service (INS), 103–104, 107
Income, 50–51
Intolerance, 93

Jackson, Jesse (Rev.), 87
Jamaicans, 82
Jews, Eastern European, 40

Kennedy, John F., 90
Key West, 18
King, Martin Luther, Jr., 74

Labor conflicts, 19–20
La Liga Contra el Cancer, 72
Latin Builders' Association, 72, 98
Latin Chamber of Commerce
  (CAMACOL), 72, 98
Laughlin, Meg, 111
Liberty City, 75
Little Haiti, 75, 79
Little Havana, 47, 87, 102, 105
Los Angeles, 2

McDermott, Jim, 113
Maceo, Antonio, 81
Maceo/King Initiative, 81
Machado, Gerardo, 20
Maidique, Modesto, 106
Mandela, Nelson, 79–80
Mas Santos, Jorge, 103

Martí, José, 17, 19, 34, 36, 117
Martínez Ybor, Vicente 18–19
Meeks, Carrie, 81
Mesa Redonda, 113
Metro Miami Action Plan, 75
Metropolitan Dade County
  Commission, 81
Mexicans, 78, 82
Miami, 27, 40, 42, 45–55, 63, 68,
  79–80, 87, 98, 103, 105, 113,
  118, 120
Miami Beach, 75–76, 79–80
Miami-Dade, County of, 49, 78, 88,
  96, 98, 107
  Community Relations Board
    of, 81
  ethnic composition of, 82
Miami Herald, 2, 107, 110–111
Miami Syndrome, 7
Miami Times, 78–79
Middle East, migration from, 40
Mills, C. Wright, 4
Modernization, 58–59, 66
Munero, Lázaro, 101
Music, 43

National Association for the
  Advancement of Colored
  People (NAACP), 81
National Organization for
  Women, 80
New Jersey, 2, 95
New York City, 2, 15–17, 18
Nicaraguans, 82
Non-Group, 113

O'Brien, William, 106
Opa Locka, 81
Ortiz, Fernando, 35, 37, 39
Overtown, 76

Penelas, Alex, 96–98, 104, 110, 111
Pepper, Claude, 98
Pérez, Lisandro, 3, 8–11
Pitts, Otis, 75

Platt Amendment, 19
Politics, electoral, 95–98
    exile ideology and, 88
    Reagan candidacy and, 90–91
Portes, Alejandro, 3
Puerto Ricans, 78, 82

Qué Pasa USA?, 60–61

Race, 38–39
    socioeconomic status and, 39
Radio and TV Martí, 91
Radio stations in Miami, 72, 85,
    87, 114
Reagan, Ronald, 90, 98
Reeves, Garth, 110
Remittances, 86, 94
Reno, Janet, 77, 103, 106, 110, 114
Republican Party, 87, 89
Retirement, 63
Rieff, David, 48
Roberts, Bip, 85
Ros-Lehtinen, Ileana, 98
Rumbaut, Rubén, 3

Santiago, Fabiola, 111
Sartre, Jean-Paul, 29
Secularism, 40–42, 66
Slavery, 38–39
Small Business Administration,
    53, 75
Smith, H. T., 80
Spain
    importance in Cuban culture,
        36–37
    migration from, 36–37
Spanish American League Against
    Discrimination (SALAD), 81

Spanish-Cuban-American War, 17
Sports, 20, 34, 85–86
Stepick, Alex, 3
Sugar revolution, 38
Sweetwater, 98

Teele, Arthur, 95–97, 112
Three-generation household, 61–62
Transculturation, 35, 39

United Brotherhood of Carpenters,
    46
United Negro College Fund, 81
United States
    influence in Cuba, 32–33
    policy toward Cuba, 90–92
United Way of Dade County, 73
University of Miami, 53

Valdés, Jorge, 96
Varela, Félix, 15–16, 27, 117
Vizcon, Roberto, 111

Warshaw, Donald, 106
West Indies, migration from, 40, 82
West Miami, 98
White Americans in Miami, 72–74
Women
    employment of, 51, 63–65, 68
    households headed by, 51, 66–67
    income of, 51
    migration of, 59–60
    1940 Constitution and, 59

Ybor City, 19–20